Diet recommendations for TCM - Spleen - Qi deficiency

Please check these recommendations always with a TCM nutrition consultant, therapist, doctor or dietician. The recipes and the list of ingredients are supporting also the conventional medical therapy. The calorie disclosures of fresh ingredients (fruit and vegetables) vary according to quality and time of harvest. The contents were checked by a dietician and a nutrition consultant for the Traditional Chinese Medicine (TCM).

Author:
©2017 Josef Miligui
www.ebns.at

Source:
The lists are created from the EBNS database for nutritional counseling. The database is used by dietitians, therapists and doctors for advising the patient / client.

Literature:
The specialist literature and the training documents of the German and Austrian dietary and traditional Chinese medicine serve as a knowledge base. We have used the documents as a basis of knowledge, adapted it to our experience and completed them.
http://di-book.com

Title Photo:
©2008 Erika Weixlbaumer

Production and publishing:
BoD – Books on Demand, Norderstedt
ISBN: 9783752861372

Diet recommendations for TCM - Spleen - Qi deficiency

1   Treatment strategy

Strengthen spleen qi, move stomach qi and bring it up.
Warm / neutral / refreshing - little, hot / cold - no

2   Avoid

Bad diet style, cold drinks, no meat 4 hours before sleep, too much bread, cereals, too much raw food, cold food / drinks, milk products, tropical fruits, fruit juices, denatured food, factory sugar, fried, breaded and fat.

3 Breakfast

4 Snack

5 Lunch

6 Afternoon

7 Dinner

8 Any time

9 Recipes

(recommendable) = You can use more.
(little) = You should use less than specified or omit.

9.1 8 treasures of rice

Strengthens kidney and bladder, builds up Qi, strengthens the spleen, repels moisture, reduces internal heat, prevents cancer, builds heart, calms nerves.
Cooking time approx. 1 hour
Calories p. portion: 212
4 portions

Quantity of ingredients
Lily bulbs 1 table spoon / 5g. (recommended).................................*
Longane 1 table spoon / 5g. (yes) ....*
King Solomon's-seal 1 table spoon / 5g. (recommended)................*
Yam root, yam root tuber 1 table spoon / 5g. (recommended)..........*
Coix (seeds) YiYi Ren 1 table spoon / 5g. (little) ....*
Rice wild (nature rice) 1 1/2 cups / 240g. (yes) ....metal
Water 8-10 cups / 800g. (yes) .... earth

Cooking instructions:
Each one 1 tbsp: Bai He, Longan, Yu Zhu, Da Zao, Shan Yao, Lian Mi, Yi Yi Ren, Qian Shi

Add hot water and soak for about 30 minutes. Then add 1 - 2 cups of rice (normal) and simmer for 1/2 to 1 hour until the rice is very soft. Or: Cook for about 3 hours with the herbs a congee. Then the herbs do not have to be soaked.

9.2 Adzuki Bean and Rice Soup

Reduces moisture, directs down, reduces gastrointestinal heat, builds up essence, strengthens muscles after heat illness, builds up body fluids.
Cooking time approx. 2 hours
Calories p. portion: 199
1 portions

Quantity of ingredients
Adzuki beans 8 table spoons / 40g. (little)..................................water
Rice round grain 2 table spoons / 20g. (recommended)............metal
Water 1 1/2 cups / 200g. (yes).. earth
Honey 1 table spoon / 8g. (little).. earth

Cooking instructions:
Boil soaked adzuki beans and round grain rice in a ratio of 4: 1 in water
until a thin pulb has formed. Sweet as needed; possibly puree.
Effect: This recipe strengthens kidney, spleen and stomach and is
particularly suitable for mothers with too little milk flow.

9.3 Andalusian fish pot

Strengthens Qi from spleen and kidneys, directs down, relaxes, builds
up Qi.
Cooking time approx. 30 min
Calories p. portion: 348
4 portions
Allergens: ADLO

Quantity of ingredients
Basic recipe for a vegetable soup 2 cups / 500g. (recommended)......*
Onion (spring onion) 2 pieces / 40g. (yes) ....metal
Olive oil 1 table spoon / 20g. (little)... earth
Lemon peel 1/2 piece / 3g. (little)... fire
Bay leaf 1 piece / 1g. (recommended) ....*
Potato 5/8 oz / 200g. (yes) .... earth
Cod 3/4 lbs / 300g. (yes) ....water
White wine 4 table spoons / 80g. (yes) ....wood
Lemon juice 1/2 teaspoon / 10g. () ....wood
Salt 1 pinch / 1g. (recommended)..water
Pepper (ground) 1 pinch / 0,2g. (recommended)......................metal
Parsley 1 table spoon / 15g. (recommended)............................wood
White bread (wheat bread) 8 slices / 250g. (recommended) ......wood

Cooking instructions:
Boil the vegetable broth with small spring onion, olive oil, grated lemon
peel and bay leaf. Boil covered for 10 minutes. Add the peeled, diced
potatoes and boil in about 8 minutes. Add fish pieces and white wine
and switch to small heat. In the slightly boiling broth put the fish and boil
it a few minutes. Season with lemon juice, salt and pepper. Serve with
parsley sprinkled. White bread as a side dish.

9.4 Apple sauce with raisins

Nourishes fluids, reduces stomach heat, strengthens spleen,
harmonizes stomach, moisturizes, relaxes, builds up Qi.
Cooking time approx. 25 min
Calories p. portion: 74
10 portions
Allergens: O

Quantity of ingredients
Apple (sweet) 2,2 lbs / 1000g. (yes)... earth
Water 1/2 cup / 100g. (yes) .... earth
Raisins 1/8 lbs - 2oz / 50g. (recommended).............................. earth

Cooking instructions:
Wash, peel and quarter the apples and remove the core. Put the apples
with the water in a pot. Wash the raisins with hot water and add them.
Cook at low heat for about 10 minutes, then allow to cool. For children
up to 10 months, mash in the blender finely. For the larger ones, crush
with the potato steamer. Fill and seal in a freezer or empty yoghurt jug.
Close the yoghurt jug. Freeze in the shock freezer.
If necessary, thaw at room temperature for about 6 hours. (Lasting
about 4 months).

The fruit mousse is intended as dessert or intermediate meal. It has an
anti-digestive effect. In case of diarrhea give better banana.

9.5 Basic recipe for a beef broth (clear)

Strengthens Qi and Yang, is very warming.
Cooking time approx. 4-8 hours
Calories p. portion: 114
10 portions
Allergens: O

Quantity of ingredients
Beef soup meat 1,1 lbs / 500g. (recommended)........................ earth
Beef meatbones 5/8 oz / 200g. (yes) .... earth
Vinegar (Red wine vinegar) 1 dash / 3g. (little) .... wood
Juniper berry 8 pieces / 6g. (recommended).............................. fire
Rosemary 1 pinch / 1g. (recommended) .... fire
Carrot 3 pieces / 210g. (recommended).................................... earth
Parsnip 2 pieces / 300g. (recommended) .... fire
Leek 1 piece / 200g. (yes) ....metal

Ginger fresh 1/2 teaspoon / 5g. (little)..metal
Lovage 1 stem / 15g. (recommended) ....metal
Clove 2 pieces / 2g. (recommended) ....metal
Pimento 6 pieces / 12g. (little) ....metal
Anise (Common Fennel) 2 pieces / 1g. (recommended) .... earth
Salt 1 teaspoon / 5g. (recommended)......................................water
Water 3,3 lbs / 1300g. (yes) .... earth

Cooking instructions:
Heat water, a dash of red wine vinegar, some juniper berries, a little
rosemary, bones and meat till it boils; add carrot, parsnip, leek, ginger,
lovage, clove, allspice, star anise and a little salt; simmer for 4-8 hours
then strain.
Refrigerate for later use.

9.6   Basic recipe for a chicken broth worming

Strengthens Qi and blood, is very warm.
Cooking time approx. 2-3 hours
Calories p. portion: 90
9 portions
Allergens: L

Quantity of ingredients
Chicken meat 1/2 piece / 600g. (recommended)......................wood
Carrot 2 pieces / 150g. (recommended)................................... earth
Leek 1 stick / 45g. (yes) ....metal
Celery root 1 piece / 500g. (recommended)............................ earth
Ginger fresh 2 slices / 2g. (little) ....metal
Fenugreek 1 teaspoon / 2g. (recommended) ....*
Juniper berry 1 teaspoon / 3g. (recommended)........................... fire
Bay leaf 3 pieces / 2g. (recommended) ....*
Water 4 cup / 900g. (yes).. earth

Cooking instructions:
Remove chicken parts from fat. Place chicken pieces in a saucepan
with hot water and heat till it boils briefly, skimming any resulting foam.
Add coarsely chopped vegetables and all spices and cook over medium
heat for 2 to 3 hours. Strain the finished soup. Throw away vegetables
and bones.
Tip: If you want to use the meat as a soup insert, take out after 45
minutes and return only the bones in the soup.
Refrigerate for later use.

9.7 Basic recipe for a reissue soup (Congee)

Warms the stomach and spleen, harmonizes the intestine, forces Qi, reduces moisture.
Cooking time approx. 2-4 hours
Calories p. portion: 140
3 portions

Quantity of ingredients
Rice variety any 1 cup / 120g. (recommended)..........................metal
Water 6 cups / 700g. (yes) .... earth

Cooking instructions:
Cook rice and water in a ratio of about 1: 6. The amount of water determines the thickness of the mash (matter of taste).
Put the rice in a saucepan with a heavy lid. It is important to simmer the rice after a short boil on the slightest flame, otherwise it burns.
Boil the rice for 2-4 hours. The longer he cooks, the more he strengthens.
If you want to eat the dish for breakfast, you can put the rice on just before bedtime.
To be on the safe side, you should first check the behavior of your pot and cooker under observation for a similar amount of time, so that nothing burns.
Refrigerate for later use.

9.8 Basic recipe for a vegetable soup, nutritious

Strengthens spleen and lung, regulates Qi flow, builds up Qi, dries out, passes downwardly, strengthens stomach Qi.
Cooking time approx. 2-3 hours
Calories p. portion: 48
5 portions
Allergens: L

Quantity of ingredients
Olive oil 1 table spoon / 4g. (little).. earth
Onion white 1 piece / 60g. (yes) ....metal
Carrot 3 pieces / 200g. (recommended).................................... earth
Parsnip 3/8 lbs - 6oz / 150g. (recommended) .... fire
Celery root 1 cup / 100g. (recommended)................................. earth
Ginger fresh 1/2 teaspoon / 2g. (little)......................................metal
Lemon 1/2 piece / 25g. ().. wood
Juniper berry 6 pieces / 6g. (recommended)............................... fire

Thyme dried 1 pinch / 1g. (recommended) ....metal
Lovage 1 table spoon / 3g. (recommended)............................metal
Bay leaf 2 leaves / 1g. (recommended) ....*
Salt 1 pinch / 1g. (recommended)..water
Water 3 cups / 650g. (yes) .... earth

Cooking instructions:
Cut the vegetables into cubes.
Heat oil in hot pot, fry shortly onions and vegetables.
Add cold water, then add ginger, bay leaf and lemon juice.
Season with juniper, thyme and lovage. Cover for 2 - 3 hours on a low heat and simmer.
The used vegetables should be thrown away.
The basic recipe serves as a soup base and to refine vegetables, legumes or cereals.
If you want to eat vegetable soup immediately, add the desired vegetables half an hour before.
Refrigerate for later use.

9.9   Bean paste piquant sweet

Strengthens spleen, stomach and kidney, strengthens middle as well as kidneys Jang, Yin and Jing.
Cooking time approx. 1 hour
Calories p. portion: 311
1 portions
Allergens: MO

Quantity of ingredients
Black beans 1 cup / 120g. (little)..water
Ginger fresh 1 inch / 3g. (little)...metal
Boxhorn clover seeds 1/2 teaspoon / 2g. (recommended)...............*
Tomato paste 1 table spoon / 10g. (recommended)...................wood
Olive oil 2 table spoons / 20g. (little) .... earth
Pumpkin seed oil 1 dash / 3g. (little) .... earth
Mustard 1 knife tip / 1g. (recommended)..................................metal
Radish horseradish 1 teaspoon (grated) / 2g. (yes)...................metal
Pepper (ground) 1 pinch / 0,5g. (recommended)......................metal
Garlic 2 cloves / 3g. (little) ....metal
Salt 1 pinch / 1g. (recommended)..water
Sugar molasses 2 table spoons / 20g. (yes) .... earth
Lemon peel 1/2 piece / 1g. (little)... fire

Cooking instructions:
Boil beans (with spices and ginger), drain water and puree. Season with spices.

Refine with sugar beet syrup and lemon peel.

9.10 Beef broth

Warming and nourishing, builds up Qi, strengthens blood and fluids.
Cooking time approx. 2-6 hours
Calories p. portion: 125
7 portions
Allergens: L

Quantity of ingredients
Water 4 cup / 1000g. (yes) .... earth
Lemon 2 dashes / 2g. () .... wood
Beef meat 1,1 lbs / 500g. (recommended) .... earth
Beef meatbones 2 pieces / 0g. (yes).. earth
Turmeric (yellow root) 1 pinch / 1g. (recommended) ....*
Carrot 2 pieces / 100g. (recommended)................................... earth
Celery root 1 inch / 25g. (recommended)................................. earth
Parsley root 1 piece / 150g. (recommended) .... earth
Onion white 1 piece / 50g. (yes) .... metal
Bay leaf 2-3 leaves / 2g. (recommended) ....*
Coriander 1/2 teaspoon / 2g. (recommended)........................... metal
Ginger fresh 1 inch / 2g. (little).. metal
Wakame 1 inch / 1g. () .... water
Parsley 1 stem / 10g. (recommended) .... wood

Cooking instructions:
In a saucepan with water (enough to cover the meat), add a few drops
of lemon juice, a little turmeric, beef and bones, heat till it boils and
simmer for a while; then pour away the whole broth, clean the pot, rinse
off meat and bones with hot water (this will save you from foaming) and
put it back to the saucepan with hot water (amount as you like); add a
good pinch of turmeric, carrot, celery, parsley root to the pot; add onion,
bay leaves, coriander, a piece of sliced ginger, a strip of wakame, a
stalk of parsley; boil everything together and simmer for 2-6 hours (if the
meat is to be used otherwise, take it out of the broth after 1 1/2 - 2
hours, as soon as it is cooked, the bones are returned to the broth);
When the cooking time is over, pour the broth through a sieve and
discard all ingredients.

Notes: The longer the broth has cooked, the warmer but more nourishing it is. It is after cooling for 3-4 days in the refrigerator durable. The broth can be drunk hot or used as a base for soups with cereals, potatoes and fresh vegetables.

9.11 Beef soup with carrots, leeks, bay leaves

Strengthens spleen Qi, strengthens blood and Qi, moisturizes, relaxes, builds up Qi, spreads, strengthens spleen and liver, regulates Qi flow, strengthens stomach Qi.
Cooking time approx. 2-3 hours
Calories p. portion: 194
5 portions

Quantity of ingredients
Beef meat 1 lbs / 500g. (recommended) .... earth
Carrot 2 pieces / 200g. (recommended) .... earth
Leek 1/2 piece / 150g. (yes) ....metal
Bay leaf 3 leaves / 1g. (recommended) ....*
Corn Grease (Polenta) 1 table spoon / 10g. (recommended) ..... earth
Water 2 cup / 450g. (yes) .... earth
Salt 1 pinch / 0,5g. (recommended) ....water

Cooking instructions:
In a saucepan with water (enough to cover the meat), add beef soup meat or leg slice and simmer for a moment; then pour off the broth, rinse the meat with hot water (this will save you from foaming), clean the pot and put the meat in hot water again; add chopped carrot, leek, corn and bay leaf; simmer until the meat is cooked.

9.12 Beef soup with colorful vegetables and mushrooms

Nourishing and slightly warming, builds up Qi and fluids, strengthens spleen Qi, strengthens blood and Qi, relaxes, builds up Qi, spreads, moves Qi and blood, diuretic, nourishes lung Yin, produces humors.
Cooking time approx. 2-6 hours
Calories p. portion: 142
6 portions
Allergens: EO

Quantity of ingredients

Water 3 cups / 700g. (yes) .... earth
Lemon 1 dash / 2g. () .... wood
Pepper powder (hot) 1 pinch / 0,3g. (recommended) .... fire
Beef meat 1,1 lbs / 500g. (recommended) .... earth
Broccoli 1 cup cutted / 100g. (yes) .... earth
Kohlrabi 1 cup diced / 100g. (recommended) .... earth
Ginger fresh 1 inch / 3g. (little) .... metal
Oregano fresh 2 table spoons / 6g. (recommended) .... metal
Soy sauce 1 dash / 1g. (little) .... water
White wine 2 table spoons / 20g. (yes) .... wood
Oyster mushroom 4-6 pieces / 20g. (little) .... earth
Chinese cabbage 3-4 table spoons (cut) / 30g. (yes) .... earth
Pepper (ground) 1 pinch / 0,2g. (recommended) .... metal
Onion (spring onion) 2-3 pieces / 50g. (yes) .... metal
Salt 1 pinch / 0,5g. (recommended) .... water

Cooking instructions:

Heat in a saucepan with water (enough to cover the meat), a dash of lemon juice, a pinch of rose paprika, beef stew or leg slice, till it boils and simmer for a moment; then pour off the broth, rinse the meat with hot water (this will save you from foaming), clean the pot and put the meat in hot water again; chopped stalks of broccoli, chopped kohlrabi, a piece of sliced ginger; simmer until the meat is cooked; abundant dried oregano,
Add soy sauce, white wine or lemon juice, some rose paprika or fresh oregano, oyster mushrooms cut into strips or shiitake mushrooms, add the broccoli florets, chopped Chinese cabbage; simmer until the ingredients are cooked; ground pepper, add plenty of chopped green onions; simmer briefly, season with salt, lemon juice.

9.13 Beluga lentil stew with vegetables

Tonifies Qi and blood, forces kidneys and spleen, dissipates heat and moisture.
Cooking time approx. 20 min
Calories p. portion: 201
5 portions

Quantity of ingredients

Lentils 1 1/2 cups / 240g. (little) .... water
Water 4-5 cups / 500g. (yes) .... earth
Carrot 3 pieces / 150g. (recommended) .... earth

Leek 1 piece / 300g. (yes)...metal
Kohlrabi 1/2 piece / 200g. (recommended) ....earth
Tomato 2 pieces / 80g. ()...wood
Onion white 1 piece / 50g. (yes) ....metal
Bay leaf 2 leaves / 1g. (recommended) ....*
Fennel 1 piece / 250g. (recommended) ....earth
Star anise 2 pieces / 1g. (recommended) ....*
Juniper berry 6 pieces / 2g. (recommended)...............................fire
Olive oil 2 table spoons / 30g. (little)..earth
Salt 1 pinch / 1g. (recommended)..water
Ginger fresh 1/2 teaspoon / 2g. (little).....................................metal
Black caraway 1 pinch / 1g. (recommended) ....*

Cooking instructions:
Heat oil in hot pot. Fry onions and add diced vegetables and spices, lentils (washed well) and salt. Cover with cold water (3 fingers wide) and cook for 20 minutes on a low heat.
Sprinkle with fresh herbs and black cumin
Goes well with rice!

9.14 Black-eyed beans stew

Strengthens spleen and kidney, is very nutritious, warms the stomach and spleen, harmonizes the intestine, forces Qi, strengthens stomach and kidney, strengthens spleen and kidney.
Cooking time approx. 20 min
Calories p. portion: 140
5 portions

Quantity of ingredients
Black-eyed peas 1 cup / 100g. (little)...water
Rice variety any 1 1/2 cups / 200g. (recommended) ....metal
Water 10 cups / 1000g. (yes)..earth

Cooking instructions:
Soak the beans overnight and strain.

In a ratio of 1: 2, simmer the beans together with the rice in the Water. Depending on how hot the flame is and how thin the dish should be, more water must be added.

Variation: Add vegetables fried in oil, such as carrots, celery tubers, onions or leeks.

9.15 Boiled fillet with potatobiscuits (Austrian Tafelspitz)

Strengthens spleen Qi, strengthens blood and Qi, moisturizes, relaxes, builds up Qi, spreads, forces Qi, forces spleen, relieves inflammation, moisturizes.
Cooking time approx. 3 hours
Calories p. portion: 454
8 portions

Quantity of ingredients
Onion white 1 piece / 50g. (yes)..metal
Corn germ oil 1 table spoon / 10g. (recommended)................... earth
Water 32 cup - 1 gallon / 0g. (yes)...................................... earth
Beef meat 5,4 lbs - 70oz cap of rump / 1800g. (recommended). earth
Beef meatbones 4n slices with bone marrow / 0g. (yes)............. earth
Salt 1 pinch / 0,5g. (recommended)......................................water
Peppercorns 15 pieces / 0g. (recommended) ....metal
Parsnip 1 piece / 0g. (recommended)... fire
Carrot 2 pieces / 0g. (recommended) .... earth
Celery root 1 slice / 0g. (recommended) .... earth
Parsley root 2 pieces / 0g. (recommended)............................... earth
Leek 1/2 stick / 0g. (yes) ....metal
Chives 1 table spoon (chopped) / 7g. (recommended).............. metal
Potato 2,2 lbs / 1000g. (yes)... earth
Sunflower oil 2 table spoons / 20g. (little)............................... earth
Salt 1 pinch / 0,5g. (recommended).....................................water

Cooking instructions:
Halve the onions, but do not peel. Brown onions in a pan with fat on the cut surfaces very dark. Wash meat and bones briefly with warm water, drain.
Heat the water till it boils, put in meat and cook gently. Always scoop up rising foam. As soon as no more foam rises, add peppercorns and the onion. Clean and cut root and leeks and add after about two and a half hours cooking time. Simmer for another half hour.
Remove boiled beef from the soup, pour through a sieve and season with salt. Cut roots into bite-sized pieces. Add the soup together with the marrow bones and leave it under the boiling point. Cut the boiled beef into finger-thick slices against the grain, place in the soup, heat again, sprinkle with a little chives.
In addition, cook and peel the potatoes in salted water. Stomp roughly or cut finely. Fry in a pan with the oil crispy.

9.16 Carp soup

Nourishing and slightly warming, strengthens the middle and the lower heater, removes moisture.
Cooking time approx. 2 hours
Calories p. portion: 499
2 portions
Allergens: DO

Quantity of ingredients
Carp 1,1 lbs / 500g. (recommended) ....water
Salt 1 pinch / 1g. (recommended)...water
Vinegar (Apple vinegar) 1 teaspoon / 3g. (little) ....wood
Thyme 1 Twig / 3g. (recommended) .... *
Juniper berry 8 pieces / 3g. (recommended)................................ fire
Carrot 2 pieces / 200g. (recommended).................................... earth
Leek 1 piece / 200g. (yes) ....metal
Onion white 1 piece / 60g. (yes) ....metal
Ginger fresh 1/2 teaspoon / 2g. (little)......................................metal
Bay leaf 3 leaves / 1g. (recommended) .... *
White wine 1/2 cup / 125g. (yes)..wood
Basil 3 leaves / 1g. (recommended)..metal

Cooking instructions:
Preparation: When shopping at the fishmonger, remove the fillets from a medium-sized, whole carp and also pack the fish head, spine with bones and tail.

Cut the fillets into 1 cm cubes; salt and set aside.

Place fish head, backbone and tail of carp in plenty of cold water; heat till it boils and scoop the foam; add a dash of vinegar, a fresh sprig of thyme, juniper berries; Add carrot, a piece of leek and chopped onion; add a thick slice of ginger, some peppercorns, 1 bay leaf, salt; simmer for about 1 1/2 hours and pour the stock through a sieve.

Put the carp pieces in a saucepan; pour a shot of white wine; Add rose paprika, basil leaves, finely ground carrots, dried thyme and the stock and warm; Boil the ingredients for about 5 minutes until the fish pieces are cooked.
Variants: Thicken the soup with kuzu or mashed potatoes.
This fits: baguette and dry white wine.

9.17 Carrot and rice gruel soup

Warms the stomach and spleen, harmonizes the intestine, forces Qi, reduces moisture, strengthens spleen and liver, regulates Qi flow, moisturizes, relaxes, builds up Qi, spreads.
Cooking time approx. 10 min
Calories p. portion: 101
1 portions

Quantity of ingredients
Basic recipe for a rice soup (Congee) 1 cup / 120g. (recommended) *
Carrot 2 pieces / 100g. (recommended).................................... earth
Salt 1 teaspoon / 4g. (recommended)......................................water

Cooking instructions:
Peel and grate carrots. Heat the rice soup (according to the basic recipe) till it boils and add the grated carrots and salt. Cook for 10 minutes.

9.18 Carrot Risotto

Forces stomach, spleen and liver, regulates Qi flow, relaxes, builds up Qi, spreads, dries out, passes downwardly, strengthens stomach Qi, nourishes blood and liver, harmonizes liver and spleen, forces eyesight, preserves the fluids, contracts.
Cooking time approx. 45 min
Calories p. portion: 308
2 portions
Allergens: GL

Quantity of ingredients
Olive oil 1/2 teaspoon / 5g. (little).............................. earth
Onion (spring onion) 2 table spoons / 7g. (yes)........................metal
Nutmeg 1 pinch / 0,3g. (recommended)...................................metal
Parsley 1/2 bunch / 25g. (recommended) ....wood
Rice variety any 1/4 lbs - 4oz / 100g. (recommended) ....metal
Carrot 5/8 lbs - 8oz / 250g. (recommended)............................ earth
Basic recipe for a vegetable soup 1 cup / 280g. (recommended) ....*
Fennel seeds ground 1/4 teaspoon / 1g. (yes)......................... earth
Basil (fresh) 1/2 teaspoon / 2g. (recommended) ....metal
Salt 1 pinch / 1g. (recommended)..water
Pepper (ground) 1 pinch / 0,3g. (recommended)......................metal
Parmesan 1 table spoon / 10g. (little) .... earth

Cooking instructions:
Heat the oil in a pan, fry the onions in a glassy and very soft manner. Add parsley, sauté briefly. Add rice, carrots and nutmeg, sauté briefly while stirring. Add the vegetable stock, season with fennel and basil, heat till it boils and cook for about 20 minutes until the rice and carrots are well. Stir from time to time and add some vegetable stock if necessary. The risotto should be slightly soupy. Just before the end of the cooking time mix in the white wine and simmer the risotto for a short while. Remove risotto from the heat, mix in Parmesan.

9.19 Celery juice

Strengthens stomach Qi, moisturizes, relaxes, builds up Qi, spreads.
Cooking time approx. 5 min
Calories p. portion: 33
1 portions
Allergens: L

Quantity of ingredients
Celery root 1/2 piece / 200g. (recommended) .... earth
Water 1 cup / 120g. (yes) .... earth
Salt 1 pinch / 0,5g. (recommended) .... water

Cooking instructions:
Peel celeriac and cut into pieces and juice. Mix with water and salt as needed.

9.20 Champignon rice

Strengthens spleen, builds up Qi, directs heat down, strengthens stomach Qi, cools blood heat.
Cooking time approx. 30 min
Calories p. portion: 410
2 portions
Allergens: L

Quantity of ingredients
Onion white 1 piece / 50g. (yes) .... metal
Bay leaf 2 pieces / 1g. (recommended) .... *
Clove 2 pieces / 1g. (recommended) .... metal
Basic recipe for a vegetable soup 7/8 lbs / 350g. (recommended) ...... *
Rice (whole grain) 5/8 oz / 200g. (recommended) .... metal
Champignon 1/8 lbs - 2oz / 60g. (little) .... earth
Parsley 1/2 oz / 20g. (recommended) .... wood

Pepper (ground) 1 pinch / 0,2g. (recommended)........................metal

Cooking instructions:
Plug in the cloves in the onion. Heat the vegetable stock with the onion and the bay leaves till it boils. Add the rice to the boiling liquid, reduce the temperature to the lowest level and stir with the lid closed for 20-25 minutes.
In the meantime, wash the mushrooms, clean them, slice them, sauté briefly with a little water or sauté. Wash the parsley and chop finely.
Remove the onion from the rice, add the mushrooms and the parsley, season with pepper.

9.21 Chicken in an ilalian style

Forces Qi, blood and Jing, middle heater, builds up spleen and stomach, nourishes Qi, forces essence, preserves the fluids, moisturizes.
Cooking time approx. 1 hour
Calories p. portion: 410
4 portions
Allergens: M

Quantity of ingredients
Olive oil 2 table spoons / 30g. (little).. earth
Chicken meat 1 piece / 700g. (recommended)..........................wood
Garlic 3 cloves / 5g. (little)...metal
Rosemary 1/2 teaspoon / 2g. (recommended)............................ fire
Salt 1 pinch / 1g. (recommended)...water
Pepper (ground) 1 pinch / 0,5g. (recommended).......................metal
Water 1 cup / 20g. (yes).. earth
Rice Basmati 1 cup / 120g. (yes)..metal
Water 6 cups / 400g. (yes) .... earth
Salt 1 pinch / 1g. (recommended)...water
Lettuce 1 piece / 300g. (little)... fire
Olive oil 2 table spoons / 20g. (little)....................................... earth
Lemon juice 1/4 piece / 7g. () ....wood
Mustard 1 pinch / 3g. (recommended) ....metal
Salt 1 pinch / 1g. (recommended)...water
Honey 1 pinch / 2g. (little)... earth

Cooking instructions:
In a heavy pan (with lid) heat 1 tbsp of olive oil at low temperature. Add the chicken pieces and fry for a few minutes. Once they start to take on

color, add the remaining 2 tablespoons of olive oil and garlic. Turn the chicken parts in the oil and sprinkle with rosemary, salt and pepper. Pour with a little water and heat till it boils. Reduce the heat, put on the lid and stew the chicken for 35 to 45 minutes.

In between, check again and again whether there is enough cooking water, and if necessary, add 1 to 2 tablespoons of water each time.

As soon as the meat comes off the bone, spread the chicken parts on the plates, deglaze the roast residue in the braised pan with a few tablespoons of water or wine and spread over the meat as a sauce.

In the meantime, cook the rice in a saucepan with (1:6) salted water, on a low heat.

Wash and spin the lettuce, finely chop and serve in a bowl. In a small bowl, mix the olive oil, lemon juice, mustard, salt and honey well and add to the salad and add it to the salad.

9.22 Chicken soup with angelica root and buckthorn fruit

Strengthens spleen and nourishes the blood and Yin of the liver, forces Qi and blood, is very warming.
Cooking time approx. 1 1/2 hours
Calories p. portion: 77
3 portions
Allergens: LO

Quantity of ingredients
Basic recipe for a chicken soup (warming) 2 cup / 500g. (recommended)*
Angelica root 1/8 oz / 5g. (recommended) ....*
Bocksdorn fruits, goji berry dried 1/8 lbs - 2oz / 50g. .... wood

Cooking instructions:
When you cook chicken broth according to basic recipes add angelica root and bocksdorn fruits in the last 40 minutes.

Ingestion: Drink 2-3 cups of broth daily.

9.23 Chicken soup with green spelt, parsley and sake

Forces Qi and blood, is very warming, nourishes liver-blood, preserves the fluids, contracts, scatters and move Qi, moisturizes, reduces cold-evil, softens knots.
Cooking time approx. 1 1/2 hours
Calories p. portion: 150
2 portions
Allergens: AL

Quantity of ingredients
Basic recipe for a chicken soup 2 cup / 500g. (recommended) ....*
Green spelt 4 table spoons / 30g. (yes) .... wood
Parsley 2 table spoons / 14g. (recommended) .... wood
Sake 1 dash / 2g. () .... metal

Cooking instructions:
Cook the chicken broth according to the basic recipe. Add the ingredients in the soup and simmer 10 min.

9.24 Clear oxen tail soup with buckthorn fruit

Forces Qi, nourishes the liver blood, good for ocular fibrillation or dry eyes, muscle tension or calf cramps due to blood deficiency.
Cooking time approx. 1-2 hours
Calories p. portion: 217
6 portions
Allergens: O

Quantity of ingredients
Basic recipe for a beef soup (warming) 4 cup / 1000g. (yes) ....*
Beef Oxtail pieces 1,1 lbs / 500g. (recommended) .... earth
Shiitake, dried 4-5 pieces / 4g. (little) .... earth
Onion white 1 piece / 60g. (yes) .... metal
Sake 2 table spoons / 20g. () .... metal
Ginger fresh 1/2 teaspoon / 2g. (little) .... metal
Bocksdorn, goji berry dried 1 table spoon / 8g. .... wood

Cooking instructions:
Soak shiitake mushrooms. Blanch oxtail slices (This removes fat and impurities).
Cook in the beef broth for 1-2 hours.
Then add the spring onions, shiitake mushrooms, rice wine, buckthorn fruits and ginger and simmer gently.

9.25 Clear soup from goose

Forces spleen, stomach and lungs, relieves weakness, forces Qi, calms the stomach, gets Qi moving, directs upwards, strengthens spleen and liver, regulates Qi flow, moisturizes, relaxes, builds up Qi, spreads.
Cooking time approx. 2-3 hours
Calories p. portion: 334
6 portions

Quantity of ingredients
Goose parts 1,1 lbs / 500g. (yes)..metal
Carrot 1 piece / 100g. (recommended) .... earth
Onion (shallot) 1 piece / 25g. (yes)......................................metal
Leek 1 piece / 250g. (yes)..metal
Parsley 1 Twig / 4g. (recommended) .... wood
Lovage 1 Twig / 4g. (recommended) ....metal
Chervil 1 pinch / 0,2g. (recommended)..*
Water 4 cup / 1000g. (yes) .... earth
Salt 1 pinch / 0,5g. (recommended)......................................water

Cooking instructions:
Simmer goose pieces with vegetables and herbs for 2-3 hours. Sift through a fine cloth and cool. Degrease and store in the refrigerator.

9.26 Coconut soup

Forces Qi and blood, is very warming, nourishes Yin, blood and Jing, moisturizes, relaxes, builds up Qi, spreads, gets Qi moving, directs upwards, dissolves stagnation.
Cooking time approx. 20 min
Calories p. portion: 153
6 portions
Allergens: L

Quantity of ingredients
Olive oil 2 table spoons / 20g. (little) .... earth
Leek 1 piece / 200g. (yes) ....metal
Onion white 1 small / 40g. (yes) ....metal
Basic recipe for a chicken soup 4 cup / 1000g. (recommended)........*
Lime 1/2 juice / 20g. ()...wood
Coconut flakes 2 table spoons / 18g. (yes) .... earth
Coconut milk 1 cup / 250g. (yes) .... earth
Pimento 1 pinch / 0,2g. (little) ....metal
Salt (herbal) 1 pinch / 1g. (recommended)...............................water

Lemongrass 1 table spoon / 8g. (recommended)...............................*

Cooking instructions:
Pour olive oil into a pan, sauté the leek and onion, add the chicken broth, add the lemon grass, simmer for about 15 minutes, add coconut flakes and coconut milk, allspice and chili, salt with herb salt. Garnish with lemongrass.

9.27 Cod soup with tomatoes

Strengthens kidney Qi, strengthens blood and fluids, promotes urination, forces Qi from spleen and kidney, softens, passes downwardly, scatters and move Qi, moisturizes, reduces cold-evil, softens knots, nourishes liver-Yin.
Cooking time approx. 30 min
Calories p. portion: 176
4 portions
Allergens: DLO

Quantity of ingredients
Basic recipe for a fish soup 2 cup / 450g. (recommended)...............*
Cod 5/8 lbs - 8oz / 250g. (yes)...................................water
Onion (shallot) 1 piece / 20g. (yes)............................metal
Anise (Common Fennel) 1/2 teaspoon / 1g. (recommended) ..... earth
Ginger fresh 1/2 teaspoon / 1g. (little)........................metal
Olive oil 1 teaspoon / 3g. (little) .... earth
Tomato 1 piece / 50g. () ....wood
White wine 1/2 cup / 125g. (yes)...............................wood
Salt 1 pinch / 0,5g. (recommended)............................water
Pepper (ground) 1 pinch / 0,2g. (recommended)......................metal
Parsley 1 table spoon (chopped) / 5g. (recommended)..............wood

Cooking instructions:
Fry the onion, anise and freshly grated ginger in oil.
Add finely chopped tomatoes and sauté. Add a little wine and fish soup. Simmer gently for 10-15 minutes. Season with salt and pepper; Add the cod pieces and heat gently. Garnish with parsley at the end.

9.28 Compote of local fruit and dried fruit

Moisturizes lungs, cools heat, reduces lung mucus, produces humors, relaxes, builds up Qi, spreads, nourishes fluids, reduces stomach heat, forces spleen, produces essence, harmonizes stomach, dries out, passes downwardly.
Cooking time approx. 15 min
Calories p. portion: 45
4 portions

Quantity of ingredients
Apple (sweet) 1 piece / 150g. (yes) .... earth
Pear 1 piece / 150g. (yes) .... earth
Cinnamon ground 1 pinch / 0,2g. (recommended) ....*
Lemon peel 1/2 teaspoon / 2g. (little).. fire
Water 2 cup / 500g. (yes) .... earth

Cooking instructions:
Cook the apple and pear with the dried fruit until soft. Sprinkle with cinnamon and lemon zest (organic).

9.29 Curry rice with raisins and nuts

Nourishes fluids, reduces stomach heat, forces spleen, produces essence, harmonizes stomach, reduces cold-
evil, softens knots, forces kidney Yang
Cooking time approx. 30 min
Calories p. portion: 275
4 portions
Allergens: HO

Quantity of ingredients
Sunflower oil 1 table spoon / 15g. (little) .... earth
Onion white 1 piece / 50g. (yes) ....metal
Curry 1/2 teaspoon / 2g. (little) ....metal
Rice wild (nature rice) 1 cup / 120g. (yes)...................................metal
Salt 1 pinch / 1g. (recommended)...water
White wine 1/2 cup / 125g. (yes)...wood
Lemon Alternatively for white wine / g. () ....wood
Peppers powder 1 pinch / 1g. (recommended) ....*
Apple (sweet) 2 pieces / 300g. (yes)... earth
Raisins 2 table spoons / 25g. (recommended).......................... earth
Walnuts 2 table spoons / 25g. (recommended)......................... earth
Water 6 cups / 500g. (yes) .... earth

Cooking instructions:
Heat oil in a pot; fry chopped onions until glassy; add the curry and let it foam for a short time; then fry the raw rice for a few minutes over a gentle heat, stirring constantly; Salt, a dash of white wine or lemon juice, rose paprika, sweet apples chopped, raisins, chopped, roasted nuts added; pour hot water on it until well covered; simmer until the rice is cooked.

Goes well with: carrot and fennel vegetables, legumes with boiled vegetables, sliced poultry with ginger and mushrooms.

9.30 Fennel and potato gratin

Regulates Qi, warms the inside, lowers cold, forces stomach, relieves constipation, forces Yang, dissolves mucus, reduces wind, spreads. forces Qi, forces spleen, relaxes, builds up Qi, spreads.
Cooking time approx. 1 1/2 hours
Calories p. portion: 147
2 portions
Allergens: CGL

Quantity of ingredients
Fennel 5/8 oz / 200g. (recommended) .... earth
Potato 1/4 lbs - 4oz / 125g. (yes) .... earth
Basic recipe for a vegetable soup 1/2 cup / 100g. (recommended) ....*
Butter organic 1 teaspoon / 3g. () .... earth
Rice flour 2 teaspoons / 6g. (recommended) ....metal
Cream sour 10% 1 teaspoon / 3g. (recommended) ....*
Salt 1 pinch / 1g. (recommended) ....water
Sugar cane sugar 1 pinch / 1g. (little) .... earth
Chicken yolk 1 piece / 10g. (recommended) .... earth
Pepper Cayenne 1 pinch / 0,5g. (recommended) ....metal
Nutmeg 1 pinch / 0,5g. (recommended) ....metal
Parsley 1 teaspoon / 2g. (recommended) .... wood
Chives 1 teaspoon / 3g. (recommended) ....metal
Parmesan 1 teaspoon / 3g. (little) .... earth
Butter organic 1 teaspoon / 3g. () .... earth

Cooking instructions:
Cook peeled potatoes and then let cool. Wash the fennel, cut off the stems and remove any outer leaves.
Hold back fennel greens and add it to the sauce with the other herbs

later.

Steam the fennel tubers for about 15 - 20 minutes.

Then cut the potatoes and fennel into slices and place in layers in a greased baking dish.

Bring the liquid of fennel broth to the boil and bind it with flour.

Season with sea salt, cayenne pepper, sugar, nutmeg and sour cream. Allow to cool and alloy with egg yolk.

Spread the sauce over the casserole, sprinkle with parmesan and finely chopped parsley and chives. Bake at 200 °C / 392 °F in the oven for half an hour.

9.31 Fennel with roasted walnuts

Regulates Qi, warms the inside, lowers coldness, strengthens the stomach, relieves constipation, strengthens kidneys and spleen Yang, dissolves mucus, reduces wind, reduce cold evil, soften knots, strengthens stomach Qi.

Cooking time approx. 20 min

Calories p. portion: 342

4 portions

Allergens: HO

Quantity of ingredients

Fennel 4 pieces / 800g. (recommended)..................................... earth
Nutmeg 1 pinch / 1g. (recommended)....................................... metal
Ginger fresh 1/2 teaspoon / 1g. (little)..................................... metal
Salt 1 pinch / 1g. (recommended)... water
White wine 1/2 cup / 125g. (yes)... wood
Peppers powder 1 pinch / 1g. (recommended) ....*
Olive oil 2 table spoons / 40g. (little) .... earth
Walnuts 2 table spoons / 35g. (recommended)......................... earth
Water 1 1/2 cups / 220g. (yes)... earth
Corn Grease (Polenta) 1 cup / 120g. (recommended)............... earth
Salt 1 pinch / 1g. (recommended)... water

Cooking instructions:

Heat very little water in a pot; Fry the fennel in strips. Add Nutmeg, a little grated ginger, add salt, a dash of white wine, rose paprika.

Simmer until the vegetables are cooked, but still crisp; stir in a little olive oil; sprinkle with roasted walnuts.

Stir the polenta into a pot of hot water, stirring constantly, until the polenta has the desired consistency. Salt.

Pull the polenta off the fire and let it swell for about 10 minutes.

9.32 Fennel-Rice Soup

Regulates Qi, warms the inside, lowers cold, forces stomach, relieves constipation, forces Yang, dissolves mucus, reduces wind, spreads, strengthens Qi and kidney Jing, builds up Qi.
Cooking time approx. 15-20 min
Calories p. portion: 156
2 portions
Allergens: EG

Quantity of ingredients
Basic recipe for a rice soup (Congee) 1 cup / 300g. (recommended) *
Fennel 1/2 piece / 150g. (recommended) .... earth
Butter organic 1 table spoon / 15g. () .... earth
Soy sauce 1 dash / 3g. (little) ....water

Cooking instructions:
Cook the fennel softly in the rice soup according to the basic recipe.
Before serving, add a piece of butter and some soy sauce.

9.33 Grilled lamb chops with sweetpotatorpuree

Strengthens spleen and kidney Yang, forces Qi, heats middle and lower heater, builds up heart and veins, moisturizes respiratory tract, promotes stomach-spleen harmony.
Cooking time approx. 45 min
Calories p. portion: 914
2 portions
Allergens: E

Quantity of ingredients
Lamb meat 6 pieces (chops) / 300g. (yes) .... fire
Garlic 2 cloves / 3g. (little) ....metal
Rosemary 2 table spoons / 5g. (recommended) .... fire
Salt 1 pinch / 1g. (recommended) ....water
Olive oil 2 table spoons / 20g. (little) .... earth
Sweet potato 3/4 lbs / 300g. (yes) .... earth
Basil 1 table spoon / 3g. (recommended) ....metal
Soybean milk 1/4 lbs - 4oz / 100g. (yes) .... earth
Basil 1 table spoon / 3g. (recommended) ....metal
Salt 1 pinch / 1g. (recommended) ....water
Nutmeg 1 pinch / 0,5g. (recommended) ....metal
Pepper (ground) 1 pinch / 0,5g. (recommended) ....metal
Chard 2 handful / 20g. () .... earth

Spinach 2 handful / 20g. (yes).. earth
Savoy cabbage / kale 2 handful / 20g. (recommended)............. earth
White cabbage 2 handful / 20g. (recommended)....................... earth
Herbs various Handful / 10g. (yes) ....*
Olive oil 2 table spoons / 20g. (little) .... earth
Salt 1 pinch / 1g. (recommended)...water
Pepper (ground) 1 pinch / 0,5g. (recommended)...................... metal

Cooking instructions:
Lamb chops:
Preheat the oven grill to about 180°C/365°F and set the shelf to a
height, such that the chops are about 8 to 12 centimeters from the heat
source. Remove the most fat of the chops and place them in a fireproof
mold. Rub the meat first with garlic, then with the rosemary salt mixture
and spread a few teaspoons of olive oil over it.
Turn the lamb chops once so that they are covered with oil on both
sides, put them under the grill and grill on both sides for 5 to 7 minutes
or until the meat is well browned.

Mashed sweet potatoes:
Peel all sweet potatoes and cut into large cubes, boil gently in salted
water and strain. Leave to soak in the 100°C/212°F hot brook for a few
minutes. Remove the basil leaves. Puree sweet potatoes.
Approximately Boil 1/8 l soymilk with basil once, then strain a little and
strain and mix with the passed sweet potatoes. Season with salt,
pepper and nutmeg. Depending on the consistency of the puree, add a
little more milk.

Steamed leafy vegetables:
After the season chard, spinach, savoy cabbage, white cabbage, fresh
herbs and the mugwort in a pot with olive oil softly. Season with salt and
pepper

9.34 Indian Dal soup

Reduces internal heat and moisture, softens, passes downwardly,
strengthens spleen and liver, regulates Qi flow, moisturizes, relaxes,
builds up Qi, spreads, forces liver and kidney, reduces damp heat.
Cooking time approx. 30 min
Calories p. portion: 256
2 portions
Allergens: EN

Quantity of ingredients
Lentils 3/8 lbs - 6oz / 175g. (little) ....water
Sesame oil 2 table spoons / 30g. (little) .... earth
Carrot 1 piece / 100g. (recommended) .... earth
Onion (shallot) 1 piece / 15g. (yes)......................................metal
Water 1 1/2 cups / 200g. (yes).. earth
Ginger fresh 2 slices / 1g. (little) ....metal
Salt 1 pinch / 0,5g. (recommended)..water
Soy sauce 1 teaspoon / 3g. (little)..water
Parsley 1 teaspoon (chopped) / 3g. (recommended)................. wood
Thyme 1 teaspoon / 3g. (recommended) ....*
Basil 1 table spoon / 5g. (recommended)..................................metal

Cooking instructions:
Soak the lentils overnight.
in a hot pot, carrot, onion and a little ginger fry, pour water. Add the
lentils and cook until soft. Add salt or soy sauce and cook for another 10
minutes.
Stir in parsley before serving; Sprinkle thyme or basil over it.
Variant: Other herbs such as sage, rosemary or lovage allow a variety
of flavors.

9.35 Kidney bean pot with lamb and sage

Nourishes Yin from heart and kidney, strengthens spleen and kidney
Yang, forces Qi, heats middle and lower heater, dissolves stagnation,
directs upwards, moisturizes, relaxes, builds up Qi, spreads.
Cooking time approx. 1 1/2 hours
Calories p. portion: 391
4 portions
Allergens: F

Quantity of ingredients
Soybean oil 2 table spoons / 30g. (little) .... earth
Onion white 2 pieces / 120g. (yes)......................................metal
Lamb meat 5/8 oz / 200g. (yes) .... fire
Salt 1 pinch / 0,5g. (recommended)..water
Sage 4-5 leaves / 2g. (little).. fire
Rosemary 1/2 teaspoon / 2g. (recommended) .... fire
Thyme 1/2 teaspoon / 2g. (recommended) ....*
Kidney beans (red) 5/8 lbs - 8oz / 250g. (little).........................water
Water 3 cups / 750g. (yes) .... earth

Cooking instructions:
Soak kidney beans in water overnight and strain.
In a saucepan with oil, roast the onion. Dice the lamb and place in the pot.
Season with salt, sage, rosemary and thyme.
Roast lamb well and cover pot. Cook over low heat and add ten-quarters of a gallon (750ml.) of cold water after 10 minutes.
Salt again.
Heat till it boils. Add beans to it.
Simmer for at least 1 hour until the beans and meat are tender. ....-----

9.36 Kudzu soup in the morning

Moisturizes, relaxes, builds up Qi, spreads, forces stomach, harmonizes middle, reduces internal heat, detoxifies, softens, passes downwardly.
Cooking time approx. 5 min
Calories p. portion: 12
1 portions
Allergens: E

Quantity of ingredients
Water 1 cup / 250g. (yes) .... earth
Soy sauce 1 dash / 2g. (little) ....water
Umeboshi paste 1 knife tip / 2g. (recommended) ....water

Cooking instructions:
Mix kudzu with cold water and heat till it boils while stirring. Once it is glassy, remove from heat and let cool. Season with Tamari and Umeboshipaste or crushed umeboshi plums

There is always the possibility to support your stomach and intestines with this recipe, taken before the right breakfast.
A morning cure for stomach and mucous membranes. Fix the base balance.

9.37 Leek soup with almond mash

Gets Qi moving, moisten the lungs and large intestine, cools heat, preserves the fluids, contracts, forces Qi, forces spleen, relieves inflammation, moisturizes, relaxes, spreads.
Cooking time approx. 20 min
Calories p. portion: 115
4 portions
Allergens: HN

Quantity of ingredients

Water 2 cup / 480g. (yes) .... earth
Sugar cane sugar 1 pinch / 0,3g. (little) .... earth
Leek 2 pieces / 400g. (yes) ....metal
Salt 1 pinch / 0,5g. (recommended)...water
Lemon juice 1/2 piece / 15g. () ....wood
Rosemary 1 Twig / 3g. (recommended)... fire
Pepper powder (hot) Alternative to rosemary / g. (recommended). fire
Potato flour 1 table spoon / 8g. (recommended) .... earth
Almond puree 2 table spoons / 20g. (yes)................................... earth
Sesame oil few drops / 1g. (little).. earth
Pepper white (ground) 1 pinch / 0,2g. (recommended)...............metal

Cooking instructions:

Add a pinch of sugar to hot water, add chopped leeks and a pinch of
salt; simmer until the leek is half cooked; season with lemon juice, fresh
rosemary or rose paprika.

Dissolve potato flour separately in cold water; thicken the soup with it.

Add almond purée, a few drops of toasted sesame oil, pepper and
simmer until the leek is cooked.

Add mushrooms; they build up juices and soften the yangling effect of
the leeks.

9.38 Lentils and rice stew

Strengthens spleen and liver, regulates Qi flow, moisturizes, relaxes,
builds up Qi, spreads, warms the stomach and spleen, harmonizes the
intestine, forces Qi, reduces moisture, brings the liver Qi in motion,
cools heat.
Cooking time approx. 25 min
Calories p. portion: 232
3 portions
Allergens: LNO

Quantity of ingredients

Lentils 1/4 lbs - 4oz / 100g. (little) ....water
Water 5 cups / 500g. (yes) .... earth
Rice variety any 1 cup / 120g. (recommended).........................metal
Sesame oil 1 table spoon / 10g. (little)................................... earth
Carrot 2 pieces / 150g. (recommended)................................... earth
Celery sticks 2 rods / 20g. (little).. earth
Cumin (Caraway seed) 1 pinch / 0,2g. (recommended) ....metal
Salt 1 pinch / 0,5g. (recommended)..water
Vinegar (Apple vinegar) 1 dash / 2g. (little)...............................wood
Parsley 2 table spoons / 18g. (recommended)...........................wood

Cooking instructions:
Soak the dry lentils the day before.
Heat sesame oil in a hot pot; cut carrot and celery into small pieces and sauté; add rice, a pinch of cumin and lentils and heat till it boils.
If the lenses are soft, add salt; season with a little vinegar and garnish with parsley.

Variant: In summer you can omit the cumin and add fresh green peas, Chinese cabbage or celery.

9.39 Polenta with fried egg

Nourishing and slightly warming, builds up Qi, forces blood, Yin and Jing, strengthens stomach Qi, diuretic, moisturizes, relaxes, builds up Qi, spreads, gets Qi moving, forces fluids production, reduces cold-evil.
Not: in wet heat of the gallbladder.
Cooking time approx. 15 min
Calories p. portion: 410
2 portions
Allergens: CG

Quantity of ingredients

Water 1 1/2 cups / 200g. (yes)... earth
Corn Grease (Polenta) 1 cup / 120g. (recommended)............... earth
Ginger fresh 1 pinch / 0,5g. (little)..metal
Butter organic 1/2 teaspoon / 2g. () .... earth
Pepper (ground) 1 pinch / 0,2g. (recommended)......................metal
Nutmeg 1 pinch / 0,2g. (recommended)...................................metal
Salt 1 pinch / 0,5g. (recommended)..water
Lemon juice 1 dash / 1g. ()...wood
Pepper powder (hot) 1 pinch / 0,3g. (recommended) .... fire

Chicken egg 4 pieces / 250g. (yes).. earth
Chives 2 table spoons / 14g. (recommended)............................metal

Cooking instructions:
Stir in a saucepan with hot water polenta and a little ginger; swell until the polenta is cooked.
Add a piece of butter, pepper, nutmeg, salt, a few drops of lemon, a pinch of rose paprika.
Put the polenta in a fireproof bowl.
Put 1 fried egg per person on top; bake in the oven for a few minutes, so that the egg yolk is still liquid.
Sprinkle with ground pepper, finely chopped chives and a little salt.

9.40 Potato-basil soup

Strengthens stomach Qi, moisturizes, relaxes, builds up Qi, spreads, forces Qi, forces spleen, relieves inflammation, spreads, strengthens spleen and liver, regulates Qi flow.
Cooking time approx. 25 min
Calories p. portion: 96
4 portions
Allergens: L

Quantity of ingredients
Water 2 cups / 450g. (yes) .... earth
Potato 4 pieces / 200g. (yes)... earth
Carrot 2 pieces / 100g. (recommended)................................... earth
Celery root 1 piece / 500g. (recommended).............................. earth
Pepper (ground) 1 pinch / 0,5g. (recommended).......................metal
Ground 1 pinch / 1g. (recommended) .... earth
Garlic 1 clove / 3g. (little)..metal
Salt 1 pinch / 1g. (recommended)..water
Lemon 1 teaspoon / 3g. () ....wood
Basil (fresh) 1 Bunch / 50g. (recommended)............................metal
Peppers powder 1 pinch / 1g. (recommended) ....*
Sugar cane sugar 1 pinch / 1g. (little) .... earth
Olive oil 1 table spoon / 10g. (little)... earth

Cooking instructions:
Peeled and chopped 4 medium potatoes in a pot of hot water and 2 chopped medium carrots, a piece of celery root, a pinch of pepper, a pinch of ground cumin, crushed a small clove of garlic, a pinch of salt, 1 teaspoon of lemon juice, simmer until the Vegetables is soft.
Add 1 bunch finely chopped basil into one half of the soup and puree everything; stir in the other half of the basil; with rose paprika, a pinch of whole cane sugar, 1 tablespoon of olive oil or butter, freshly ground pepper, salt to taste.

9.41 Pumpkin curry

Forces lungs and spleen, diuretic, forces Qi, protects liver, warms the stomach and spleen, harmonizes the intestine, forces Qi, reduces moisture, moisturizes, relaxes, builds up Qi, spreads, nourishes blood and liver, harmonizes liver and spleen.
Cooking time approx. 20 min
Calories p. portion: 193
3 portions

Quantity of ingredients
Pumpkin 3/4 lbs / 300g. (yes) .... earth
Olive oil 2 table spoons / 30g. (little) .... earth
Coriander 1 pinch / 1g. (recommended)................................... metal
Pepper (ground) 1 pinch / 0,5g. (recommended)...................... metal
Curry 1 pinch / 1g. (little) .... metal
Water 1/4 cup / 50g. (yes) .... earth
Salt 1 pinch / 1g. (recommended).. water
Parsley 1 table spoon / 7g. (recommended)............................. wood
Cardamom 1 pinch / 1g. (recommended).......................................*
Turmeric (yellow root) 1 pinch / 1g. (recommended) ....*
Rice (whole grain) 1/2 cup / 60g. (recommended).................... metal
Water 3 cups / 300g. (yes) .... earth
Salt 1 pinch / 1g. (recommended).. water

Cooking instructions:
Heat olive oil in pan. Steam the pumpkin cut in cubes, season with cilantro, pepper and curry, simmer with a little water, salt with sea salt, add chopped parsley with cardamom and turmeric, simmer on a small fire for about 10 minutes, depending on the pumpkin, the pumpkin should still be firm.
Place the rice in salted water, bring to the boil and let it simmer over low heat for about 15 minutes.

9.42 Pumpkin soup

Forces lungs and spleen, diuretic, forces Qi, protects liver, forces Qi, forces spleen, relieves inflammation, moisturizes, relaxes, builds up Qi, spreads, strengthens spleen and liver, regulates Qi flow, moisturizes, relaxes, builds up Qi, spreads.
Cooking time approx. 1 hour
Calories p. portion: 105
3 portions

Quantity of ingredients
Pumpkin 3/4 lbs / 300g. (yes) .... earth
Carrot 2 pieces / 100g. (recommended)..................................... earth
Potato 2 pieces / 120g. (yes)... earth
Olive oil 1 table spoon / 10g. (little).. earth
Onion white 1 piece / 50g. (yes) ....metal
Water 1 cup / 120g. (yes)... earth
Parsley 1 table spoon / 7g. (recommended)............................. wood
Anise (Common Fennel) 1 pinch / 1g. (recommended) .... earth
Salt 1 pinch / 1g. (recommended)...water

Cooking instructions:
Add the olive oil to the pan, add the diced pumpkin, diced carrots and potatoes. Roast them shortly, add the finely chopped onion, fill with water, add enough water to cover the vegetables at least 3 finger-widths. Boil at low heat.

Season with sea salt, add small cutted parsley, a pinch of anise (little). Allow to simmer for about 35 minutes. Then purée the soup and add some water, depending on the consistency of the soup.

9.43 Quick flakes with compote or jam

Forces Qi, dries out, passes downwardly, strengthens middle heater, moisturizes, relaxes, builds up Qi, spreads, strengthens kidney Qi, essence and brain, forces kidney, warms the middle.
Cooking time approx. 5 min
Calories p. portion: 189
2 portions
Allergens: H

Quantity of ingredients

Quinoa 5-7 table spoons / 50g. (yes)... fire
Water 1 cup / 250g. (yes)... earth
Compote (fruits of the season) 1 cup / 100g. (recommended)...........*
Walnuts 1 table spoon (grated) / 8g. (recommended) .... earth
Olive oil 1 table spoon / 10g. (little).. earth
Honey 2 table spoons / 20g. (little) .... earth
Vanilla 1 pinch / 0,2g. (recommended) ....*
Anise (Common Fennel) 1 pinch / 0,2g. (recommended) .... earth
Cardamom 1 pinch / 0,2g. (recommended)......................................*

Cooking instructions:

Put the quinoa flakes in a pan and add water. Boil for 3-5 minutes, pull from the fire, add nuts and compote. Add a dash of oil. Sweeten as needed with honey, whole cane sugar or agave syrup.
Spices and aromas: vanilla, anise, fennel or coriander, cardamom, a little chili.

Winter: apple compote, pear compote, fruit jam.
Summer: plum compote, apricot compote.

9.44 Quinoa with peach

Strengthens blood and fluids, brings blood into motion, builds up Qi, spreads, forces Qi, dries out, passes downwardly, strengthens middle heater, moisturizes.
Cooking time approx. 20 min
Calories p. portion: 248
2 portions

Quantity of ingredients

Quinoa 1 cup / 100g. (yes) .... fire
Water 1 1/2 cups / 240g. (yes).. earth
Honey 2 teaspoons / 4g. (little)... earth
Peaches 2 pieces / 240g. (yes) .... earth
Linseed oil 2 teaspoons / 4g. (little) .... earth
Lemon Balm (fresh) 1 teaspoon (chopped) / 1g. (recommended)metal
Cinnamon ground 1 pinch / 0,2g. (recommended) ....*
Vanilla 1 pinch / 0,2g. (recommended) ....*

Cooking instructions:

In the evening: Put quinoa in hot water and boil soft, covered 15 to 20 minutes.

In the morning: Warm up quinoa with 1 tablespoon water.
Steam lightly Peaches in a saucepan or add them fresh. Decorate with fresh lemon balm.

Summer: nectarines, apricots
Winter: Pickled fruit, pear, apples

9.45 Radish with spring onions and carrots

Nutritious, moisturizing and dynamizing, moves Qi and blood, dissolves stagnation, directs upwards, strengthens stomach Qi, diuretic, moisturizes, relaxes, builds up Qi, spreads. regulates Qi, warms spleen and kidney.
Cooking time approx. 30 min
Calories p. portion: 246
2 portions
Allergens: EG

Quantity of ingredients
Carrot 2 pieces / 200g. (recommended).................................... earth
Radish black 1/2 piece / 100g. (yes)...metal
Ginger powder 1 knife tip / 0,2g. (little) ....metal
Onion (spring onion) 1 piece / 20g. (yes)..................................metal
Salt 1 pinch / 0,5g. (recommended)..water
Soy sauce 1 dash / 2g. (little) ....water
Lemon juice 2 table spoons / 16g. ()..wood
Curcuma 1 pinch / 0,2g. (recommended)...*
Pepper powder (hot) 1 pinch / 0,2g. (recommended) .... fire
Butter organic 1 teaspoon / 3g. () .... earth
Water 1 cup / 250g. (yes).. earth
Corn Grease (Polenta) 1 cup / 100g. (recommended)............... earth
Salt 1 pinch / 0,5g. (recommended)..water

Cooking instructions:
Cook finely chopped carrots, black or white finely chopped radish, a pinch of grated ginger. Steam for 10 minutes, then strain.
In the meantime stir in chopped spring onions, salt, soy sauce, a little lemon juice, a pinch of turmeric or rose paprika and a piece of butter.

Garnish:
Stir the polenta into a pot of hot water, stirring constantly, until the polenta has the desired texture. Pull the polenta off the fire and let it swell for about 10 minutes.

9.46 Reissue soup with fresh fruits

Forces kidney and bladder, strengthens Qi and kidney Jing, moisturizes, relaxes, builds up Qi, reduces internal heat, produces humors, moisturizes, spreads, expels cold, dissolves stagnation, drives sweat, stimulates nerves.
Cooking time approx. 1 1/2 hours
Calories p. portion: 143
4 portions
Allergens: G

Quantity of ingredients
Rice wild (nature rice) 1 cup / 100g. (yes)................................metal
Water 8 cups / 900g. (yes) .... earth
Apple (sweet) 1 1/2 cups / 200g. (yes)..................................... earth
Butter organic 1 table spoon / 10g. ()...................................... earth
Vanilla 1 pinch / 0,2g. (recommended) ....*
Sugar cane sugar 2 teaspoons / 6g. (little)............................... earth

Cooking instructions:
Prepare rice congee according to basic recipe.

At the end, add finely chopped fruits to the season, vanilla, chili and butter; sweet to taste.

Variant: With nuts, the dish can always be made richer and more filling.

Effect: Cooked or steamed fruits are easier to digest and act better than raw. For some fruits, which are particularly suitable for hot summer days - such as melons and berries - it is still advisable to add the fruits only to a hot porridge.
Other types of fruit - such as apples, pears, plums and cherries - can also be simmered for a while.

9.47 Reissue soup with kidneys

Forces kidney-Yang, warming, warms the stomach and spleen, harmonizes the intestine, forces Qi, reduces moisture. regulates Qi, warms spleen and kidney, dissolves stagnation, directs upwards.
Cooking time approx. 1 1/2 hours
Calories p. portion: 301
2 portions
Allergens: E

Quantity of ingredients
Rice variety any 1/2 cup / 50g. (recommended)........................metal
Beef kidney 5/8 lbs - 8 oz / 200g. (yes)................................... earth
Olive oil 2 table spoons / 20g. (little)... earth
Water 3 cups / 360g. (yes) .... earth
Ginger fresh 1/2 teaspoon / 1g. (little)..............................metal
Onion (spring onion) 2 pieces / 40g. (yes) ....metal
Fennel seeds ground 1 pinch / 0,3g. (yes).............................. earth
Pepper (ground) 1 pinch / 0,2g. (recommended)......................metal
Nutmeg 1 pinch ground / 0,2g. (recommended)........................metal
Soy sauce 1 dash / 2g. (little) ....water

Cooking instructions:
Fry finely chopped and well-cleaned kidneys in oil, ginger and spring
onions.

Cook the rice soup according to the "Basic recipe for a reissue soup
(Congee)" with 3 cups of water.

Season with ground fennel seeds, pepper, nutmeg and soy sauce.

9.48 Rice congee with carrots and fennel

Nutritious builds up Qi, forces the digestive functions.
Cooking time approx. 2 hours and more
Calories p. portion: 131
3 portions
Allergens: G

Quantity of ingredients
Basic recipe for a rice soup (Congee) 2 cup / 500g. (recommended) *
Carrot 2 pieces / 100g. (recommended).................................... earth
Fennel 1 piece / 250g. (recommended) .... earth
Butter organic 1 teaspoon / 3g. () .... earth
Cardamom 1/2 teaspoon / 1g. (recommended).............................*

Cooking instructions:
Cook rice congee according to basic recipe.
Clean and cut carrots and fennel.
When carrots and fennel are cooked from the beginning, they serve
wholesomeness. If added shortly before the end of the cooking time,
taste and vitamins are retained.
Refine with butter and cardamom before serving.

9.49 Rice congee with crushed walnuts

Nourishing and slightly warming, warms the middle, builds up Qi, warms the stomach and spleen, harmonizes the intestine, forces Qi, reduces moisture.
Cooking time approx. 2 hours and more
Calories p. portion: 406
2 portions
Allergens: H

Quantity of ingredients
Basic recipe for a rice soup (Congee) 4 cups / 500g. (recommended)*
Sugar cane sugar 2 table spoons / 20g. (little)........................... earth
Walnuts 1 cup / 70g. (recommended)....................................... earth
Cinnamon ground 1 pinch / 0,2g. (recommended) .... *

Cooking instructions:
Cook the basic recipe for rice soup (congee)
Note: The crushed walnuts can be cooked from the beginning.
Variation: Refine with sweet or spicy ingredients as you like. In particular, cinnamon, cloves, and ginger increase the warming effect and wholesomeness.

9.50 Rice congee with dried fruit

Warms the stomach and spleen, harmonizes the intestine, forces Qi, reduces moisture, nourishes blood and Yi, harmonizes lungs Qi, strengthens Qi and kidney Jing, moisturizes, relaxes, builds up Qi, spreads.
Cooking time approx. 10 min
Calories p. portion: 210
2 portions
Allergens: GO

Quantity of ingredients
Basic recipe for a rice soup (Congee) 4 cups / 500g. (recommended)*
Butter organic 1/2 teaspoon / 5g. () .... earth
Apricot dried 6 table spoons / 50g. (recommended).................. earth
Water 1/2 cup / 50g. (yes)... earth
Maple syrup 1 dash / 3g. (yes) .... earth

Cooking instructions:
Cook rice congee according to basic recipe.

Melt a small amount of butter over a low heat and briefly fry small dried fruit with 1/2 cup of water. Add the amount of rice porridge desired for the meal and heat. Serve hot and sweeten with maple syrup if necessary.
Variant: In addition fresh fruit with braise.

9.51 Rice dulse soup

Strengthens spleen and liver, regulates Qi flow, relaxes, builds up Qi, spreads, dries out, passes downwardly, strengthens stomach Qi, warms the stomach and spleen, harmonizes the intestine, forces Qi, reduces moisture.
Cooking time approx. 5 min
Calories p. portion: 190
2 portions
Allergens: L

Quantity of ingredients
Basic recipe for a rice soup (Congee) 4 cups / 500g. (recommended)*
Basic recipe for a vegetable soup (nutritious) 2 cup / 500g. (recommended)*
Dulse (seaweed) 2 table spoons / 15g. (recommended) ....water

Cooking instructions:
Worm up a portion of pre-cooked basic recipe for a ricesoupe (congee) and a portion pre-cooked basic recipe for a vegetable soup.
Bake the dulse in the oven at 220 degrees for 3 minutes. Spread the crisp dulse over the rice.

9.52 Rice noodle soup with shiitake mushrooms

Strengthens spleen and liver, regulates Qi flow, relaxes, builds up Qi, spreads, dries out, passes downwardly, strengthens stomach Qi, nourishes Yin of the lungs, stomach and colon, supports digestion, reduces internal wind.
Cooking time approx. 20 min
Calories p. portion: 66
2 portions
Allergens: L

Quantity of ingredients

Rice noodles 2 handful / 20g. (yes) ....metal
Shiitake, dried 4-6 pieces / 5g. (little).. earth
Basic recipe for a vegetable soup 1 1/2 cups / 240g. (recommended)*
Chinese cabbage 1 cup / 60g. (yes) .... earth
Lovage 1 teaspoon / 3g. (recommended) ....metal
Miso 2 table spoons / 18g. (yes)..water

Cooking instructions:

Soak rice noodles and shiitake mushrooms separately in cold water.
Heat the vegetable broth and add the soaked shiitake mushrooms cut
into strips and simmer gently. Cut Chinese cabbage into noodles, add
lovage green and rice noodles and let it steep for a while. Before
serving, stir in Miso dissolved in a little cooled water. Recommendation:
Suitable at the beginning of each meal, also for breakfast

9.53 Rice with stewed vegetables

Dissipates heat and moisture.
Cooking time approx. 20 min
Calories p. portion: 166
2 portions
Allergens: L

Quantity of ingredients

Rice variety any 1/2 cup / 60g. (recommended) ....metal
Water 3 cups / 300g. (yes) .... earth
Lemon peel 1 piece / 3g. (little).. fire
Water 1/2 cup / 0g. (yes) .... earth
Carrot 2 pieces / 180g. (recommended)................................... earth
Celery sticks 1/2 piece / 5g. (little) .... earth
Champignon 1/2 cup / 50g. (little).. earth
Cress 2 table spoons / 20g. (little) ....metal
Linseed oil 1 dash / 3g. (little)... earth

Cooking instructions:

Cook rice according to basic recipe with a piece of lemon peel.
Steam chopped carrots, celery and mushrooms until soft.
Then sprinkle with cress. Then add a dash of high quality cold oil.

9.54 Sliced lamb with rosemary potatoes

Strengthens spleen and kidney Yang and stomach Qi, relieves weakness, heats middle and lower heater, forces Qi, relieves inflammation, moisturizes, relaxes, builds up Qi, spreads.
Cooking time approx. 1 hour
Calories p. portion: 461
4 portions
Allergens: LO

Quantity of ingredients
Lamb meat 7/8 lbs - 1 lbs / 500g. (yes).. fire
Olive oil 2 table spoons / 20g. (little).. earth
Onion white 1 piece / 50g. (yes)...metal
Garlic 1 clove / 2g. (little)..metal
Nutmeg 1 pinch / 0,2g. (recommended)....................................metal
Carrot 3 pieces / 150g. (recommended)..................................... earth
Celery root 1/4 tuber / 120g. (recommended) .... earth
Rosemary 1 Twig / 3g. (recommended)....................................... fire
Savory 1 teaspoon / 2g. (recommended)..................................water
Parsley 1 table spoon / 8g. (recommended)..............................wood
Pepper powder (hot) 1 pinch / 2g. (recommended) .... fire
Red wine 1/2 cup / 125g. (yes).. fire
Salt (herbal) 1 pinch / 1g. (recommended)...............................water
Lemon juice 1/2 piece / 15g. () ....wood
Cranberry 1 table spoon / 10g. (little)......................................wood
Potato 6 pieces / 400g. (yes)... earth

Cooking instructions:
Cut the lamb into strips, cut the carrots and celery into small cubes.
Heat the olive oil in a pan, fry the lamb in it, add the cut onions and garlic, salt with herbal salt, a little water, parsley, deglaze with red wine, season with paprika and small cut rosemary, mugwort, savory, carrots and celery, turn the heat back on small Simmer for about 35 minutes. Season with pepper and nutmeg, if necessary still salt, add a little lemon juice, season with paprika, cranberries.

Cut the potatoes in half, the length of, spread a little olive oil on the cut surface, salt, sprinkle 2-3 rosemary needles on each half potato, place the potatoes on the baking sheet and bake in a preheated oven for approx. 25 minutes at 190°C/374°F.

9.55 Soup with egg yolk

Forces Qi and Yang, is very warming.
Cooking time approx. 5 min
Calories p. portion: 173
1 portions
Allergens: CO

Quantity of ingredients
Basic recipe for a beef soup (warming) 1 cup / 250g. (yes)..............*
Chicken yolk 1 piece / 25g. (recommended).............................. earth

Cooking instructions:
Warm the beef soup according to the basic recipe for a beef broth,
warm it up and jell the yolk.

9.56 Sweet polenta with peach

Nourishing and warming, harmonizes the middle.
Cooking time approx. 20 min
Calories p. portion: 330
2 portions
Allergens: GHO

Quantity of ingredients
Water 1 1/2 cups / 240g. (yes).. earth
Corn Grease (Polenta) 1 cup / 100g. (recommended)............... earth
Butter organic 1/2 teaspoon / 2g. () .... earth
Barley malt 1/2 teaspoon / 2g. (recommended)........................ earth
Cinnamon ground 1 pinch / 0,2g. (recommended) ....*
Cardamom 1 pinch / 0,2g. (recommended)....................................*
Salt 1 pinch / 0,5g. (recommended)..water
Lemon 1 dash / 1g. ()...wood
Raisins 2 table spoons / 20g. (recommended) .... earth
Apple juice (natural cloudy) until covered / 10g. (little) .... earth
Peaches 2 pieces / 240g. (yes) .... earth
Hazelnuts 2 table spoons / 20g. (recommended)...................... earth

Cooking instructions:
Heat water till it boils. Stir in the polenta with a whisk and until tender;
add some butter or cream, barley malt or maple syrup, cinnamon, some
cardamom, a pinch of salt, a few drops of lemon juice and stir well.

Separately prepare a compote:

In a hot pot, simmer raisins in some apple or apricot juice for a few minutes; add fully ripe peaches chopped and heat; pour over the polenta served on plates; sprinkle with roasted nuts as desired.

9.57 Sweet potato pancakes with basil pesto

Forces Qi, blod, Yin and Jing.
Cooking time approx. 30 min
Calories p. portion: 625
3 portions
Allergens: ACH

Quantity of ingredients
Sweet potato 4 pieces / 500g. (yes).. earth
Onion read 1/2 piece / 30g. (yes)..metal
Basil 1 table spoon / 10g. (recommended).............................metal
Chicken egg 2 pieces / 140g. (yes).. earth
Spelled wholemeal flour 3 oz / 80g. (recommended)................wood
Salt 1 pinch / 0,5g. (recommended)..water
Olive oil 1/4 cup / 20g. (little) .... earth
Salt 1 teaspoon (coarse) / 3g. (recommended).........................water
Basil Handful / 15g. (recommended)......................................metal
Parsley Handful / 15g. (recommended) ....wood
Garlic 2 cloves / 3g. (little)..metal
Walnuts 1/8 lbs - 2oz / 60g. (recommended)........................... earth
Olive oil 2 table spoons / 20g. (little) .... earth

Cooking instructions:
Sweet Potato Buffer: Wash the sweet potato thoroughly, but do not peel, and grate into a large bowl. Add onion, basil, egg and flour, mix well and sprinkle with salt. The mixture can be formed into buffers. Bake in a preheated tube on a baking tray coated with oil for 4 to 5 minutes on both sides.

Basil Pesto: Add the salt, chopped basil and parsley and crushed garlic in a small bowl and crush (if available, use the mortar). Add the grated walnuts. While stirring, add enough olive oil until the desired consistency is achieved.

9.58 Tea from cinnamon sticks

Warms the stomach and spleen, promotes blood circulation and conduction flow, relieves cold-sickness and pain.
Cooking time approx. 15 min
Calories p. portion: 2
1 portions

Quantity of ingredients
Cinnamon sticks 1/4 piece / 1g. (recommended) ....*
Water 1 cup / 125g. (yes).. earth

Cooking instructions:
A quarter of a cinnamon stick for a cup of tea. Start cold and bring to the boil. Let it sit for 15 minutes, then strain.
This tea is unsweetened and swallowed, slowly drunk. The amount is enough for one day.

9.59 Tea from ginseng

Forces heart, lungs, stomach, spleen, kidney-Qi.
Cooking time approx. 20 min
Calories p. portion: 0
4 portions

Quantity of ingredients
Ginseng 2 teabags / 4g. (recommended)..*
Water 2 cup / 500g. (yes) .... earth

Cooking instructions:
A very mild form of taking ginseng is achieved by placing it in a thermos of hot water. You can also use the root several times, not just for a pot filling. Ideally, you should have cooked the water for 10 minutes - it is then assigned to the conversion phase of fire (TCM) - and to use non-carbonated medicinal spring water, if the quality of the water on site is not good.

Ingestion: This mild ginseng tea can be drunk throughout the day for strengthening.

9.60 Tea from ground

Reduces mucus and moist heat in the liver and gallbladder, against liver Qi stagnation, spleen qi deficiency, spleen and kidney Yang-Mangel.
Cooking time approx. 10 min
Calories p. portion: 2
4 portions

Quantity of ingredients
Ground 1 teaspoon / 3g. (recommended) .... earth
Water 2 cup / 500g. (yes) .... earth

Cooking instructions:
Heat the water till it boils and put it aside. Add crushed cumin and leave for 10 min. to let go. Sweet to taste with honey. Strain when pouring.

Drink 1 cup 2 times a day.

9.61 Tea from juniper berry

Dries out, passes downwardly, activates Wei Qi.
Cooking time approx. 10 min
Calories p. portion: 10
1 portions

Quantity of ingredients
Juniper berry 1 teaspoon / 3g. (recommended)............................ fire
Water 1 cup / 125g. (yes) .... earth

Cooking instructions:
A teaspoon of dried juniper berries for a cup of tea. Start cold and bring to the boil. Let it sit for 15 minutes, then strain.
This tea is unsweetened and swallowed, slowly drunk. The amount is enough for one day.

9.62 Tea from Longane

Forces spleen, builds up lung, builds up heart, calms nerves.
Cooking time approx. 10 min
Calories p. portion: 0
4 portions

Quantity of ingredients

Longane 2 teaspoons / 4g. (yes) ....*

Water 2 cup / 500g. (yes).. earth

Cooking instructions:

Heat the water till it boils and put it aside. Add Longane and 10 min. to let go. Sweet to taste with honey. Strain when pouring.

9.63 Tea from rosemary

Dries out, passes downwardly, forces heart, lung and spleen Qi, forces liver-blood, forces heart-Yin, expels spleen heat / cold moisture, strengthens spleen and kidney Yang.
Cooking time approx. 15 min
Calories p. portion: 1
4 portions

Quantity of ingredients

Rosemary 2-4 teaspoons / 6g. (recommended) .... fire

Water 2 cup / 500g. (yes).. earth

Cooking instructions:

Heat the water till it boils and put it aside. Add rosemary and 10 min. to let go. Strain. Sweet to taste with honey.

9.64 Tea from thyme

Converts mucus, forces lungs and spleen, dries out, passes downwardly.
Cooking time approx. 10 min
Calories p. portion: 0
4 portions

Quantity of ingredients

Thyme 3 table spoons / 6g. (recommended)...................................*

Water 2 cup water / 500g. (yes)... earth

Cooking instructions:

Heat the water till it boils and put it aside. Add thyme and 10 min. to let go. Strain. Sweet to taste with honey.
Drink 2 to 3 cups daily by mouth

9.65 Thick pea soup

Nourishes Qi, diuretic, harmonizes Qi (especially in the Middle and Lower), strengthens the kidney and the defense Qi, dischars moisture.
Cooking time approx. 2-3 hours
Calories p. portion: 123
3 portions
Allergens: AN

Quantity of ingredients
Peas, green 3/8 lbs - 6oz / 150g. (yes) ....water
Water 2 1/4 cups / 550g. (yes)... earth
Sesame oil 1 table spoon / 20g. (little).................................... earth
Onion white 1/2 piece / 25g. (yes) ....metal
Ginger fresh 1/2 teaspoon / 1g. (little).......................................metal
Ground 1/2 teaspoon / 1g. (recommended) .... earth
Oat meal 1 table spoon / 15g. (recommended) ....metal
Salt 1 pinch / 1g. (recommended)..water
Parsley 1 stem / 2g. (recommended)...wood

Cooking instructions:
Soak dried peas before cooking. Sauté sesame oil, onion, a little oatmeal, ginger and cumin in a hot pot; add the peas and simmer for 2-3 hours; add salt at the end and pruée with a blender; garnish with parsley.

9.66 Vegetable potato and meat mash

Strengthens spleen and liver, regulates Qi flow, moisturizes, relaxes, builds up Qi.
Cooking time approx. 30 min
Calories p. portion: 127
2 portions

Quantity of ingredients
Potato 1/4 lbs - 4oz / 100g. (yes)... earth
Carrot (Early Carrot) 5/8 oz / 200g. (recommended) .... earth
Beef meat (calf) 1/8 lbs - 2oz / 40g. (recommended)................. earth
Apricots juice 6 table spoons / 60g. (recommended)................. earth
Rapeseed oil 1 table spoon / 6g. (little)..................................... earth

Cooking instructions:
Remove the flesh, skin, tendons and grease, wash under cool water and cut into small pieces and boil in a little water. After about 15-20 minutes, remove and puree. Wash the vegetables and potatoes, peel and cut into not too small pieces. Cook gently with a little water over a low heat for 10-20 minutes. Use the blender to chop the vegetables. Mix everything, add butter or oil and fruit juice and puree again.

Alternately use other meats such as chicken, lamb or turkey. Also change vegetables with zucchini, kohlrabi, fennel, pumpkin, parsnips and broccoli.

Also change the fruit juices. This can produce a variety of flavors.

9.67 Vegetable semolina soup

Strengthens spleen and liver, regulates Qi flow, builds up Qi, dries out, passes downwardly, reduces moisture, regulates Qi.
Cooking time approx. 20 min
Calories p. portion: 199
3 portions
Allergens: AEGL

Quantity of ingredients
Basic recipe for a vegetable soup (nutritious) 2 cup / 500g. (recommended)*
Potato 1 piece / 80g. (yes)... earth
Parsnip 1 piece / 180g. (recommended) .... fire
Carrot 1 piece / 120g. (recommended) .... earth
Celery root 3/8 lbs - 6oz / 150g. (recommended) .... earth
Kohlrabi 1/2 piece / 200g. (recommended) .... earth
Beans (green, fresh) 1/4 lbs / 100g. (recommended) ....water
Wheat semolina 2 table spoons / 24g. ().................................. wood
Lovage 1/2 teaspoon / 2g. (recommended) ....metal
Butter organic 1 table spoon / 20g. ().. earth
Soy sauce 1 teaspoon / 3g. (little)..water

Cooking instructions:
Worm the prepared vegetable soup; cook the vegetables in the soup softly. Spread some wheatgrass and let it swell. At the end, add lovage-green and a little butter and taste with soy sauce.

9.68 Warming porridge

Forces Qi and defensive power.
Cooking time approx. 10 min
Calories p. portion: 357
1 portions
Allergens: AHO

Quantity of ingredients
Oat flakes (whole grain) 6 table spoons / 60g. (recommended)..metal
Fig dried 3 pieces / 15g. (yes) .... earth
Star anise 1 piece / 1g. (recommended) ....*
Ginger fresh 1 pinch / 0,5g. (little)..metal
Water 1 cup / 120g. (yes).. earth
Maple syrup 1 table spoon / 10g. (yes).................................... earth
Walnuts 1 table spoon (chopped) / 8g. (recommended)............. earth

Cooking instructions:
Soak the dried fruit. Roast Oatmeal dry. Add dried ginger, star anise or cinnamon, a little grated ginger and boil everything with water to a mash. With maple syrup sweet. Whip grated walnuts and sprinkle before serving.

Effect: Suitable for the cold season.
Caution: Fresh ginger does not drink over a long period of time.

10 Effects of food

10.1 Use ingredients: recommendable

Acai powder
Acerola fruit nectar or powder
Agave nectar
Agrimony
Almond
Aloe juice
Amaranth Pops
Angelica root
Anise (Common Fennel)
Apple puree
Apricot dried
Apricot jam
Apricot nectar
Apricots juice
Baking powder
Banchatee (green tea)
barberry
Barley flour
Barley grass powder
Barley grouts
Barley malt
Basic recipe for a beef soup
Basic recipe for a chicken soup
(warming)
Basic recipe for a fish soup
Basic recipe for a rice soup (Congee)
Basic recipe for a vegetable soup
(nutritious)
Basil
Basil (fresh)
Bay leaf
Beans (green, fresh)
Bearberry leaf
Beef fillet
Beef heart (calf)
Beef meat
Beef meat (calf)
Beef Oxtail pieces
Beef soup meat
Beer (alcohol-free)
Beer (alcohol-reduced)
Berries of the season
Bitter Herb liqueur
Bitter Lemon
Bitter liqueur
Bitter orange peel
Black caraway
Black fungus mushroom
Blackberry dried (unripe fruit)

Blackberry jam
Blackberry leaves
Blackthorn (Sloe)
Blue mallow tee
Blueberry dried
Blueberry jam
Bocksdorn fruits (Fructus Lycii, Goji,
goji berry dried
Borage
Boxhorn clover seeds
Brazil nuts
Bread roll
Bread with carob kernel flour
Breadcrumbs (wheat bread, bread roll)
Brie cheese
Brown ale
Buckbean
Buckwheat whole grain
Butter (half fat)
Camembert
Campari
Capers in olive oil
Cardamom
Carob flour, St. john's bread
Carp
Carrot
Carrot (Early Carrot)
Carrot juice without sugar
Celery root
Cereal coffee
Chamomile tea
Channa-Dal
Chenpi (chinese tangerine bowl)
Cherry (sour)
Cherry compote
Chervil
Chervil dried
Chestnut puree
Chestnuts
Chicken Blood
Chicken egg white
Chicken meat
Chicken yolk
Chickweed
Chili (pod or ground)
Chinese pearl barley
Chives
Chocolate (Diabetic)
Chrysanthemum blossom tea

Cinnamon ground
Cinnamon sticks
Clarified butter
Clementine
Clove
Cocoa
Coconut fat
Coconut meat
Codfish
Cola drink
Cola drink (low calorie)
Compote (fruits of the season)
Coriander
Corn (fast polenta)
Corn (roasted)
Corn flour
Corn germ oil
Corn Grease (Polenta)
Corn silk tea
Corn starch
Cottage cheese
Cranberries
Cranberry
Cranberry jam
Cream (30% fat)
Cream 10% coffee cream
Cream sour 10%
Cream sour 20%
Cream sour 30%
Creamer
Crispbread
Cucumber (bitter)
Cucumber (spicy cucumber)
Cumin (Caraway seed)
Curcuma
Currant jam (black)
Currant jam (red)
Currant juice (black)
Currants (black)
Currants (red)
Daisy
Dandelion juice
Dashi
Dates dried
Dates red
Deer's Bones
Deer's kidneys
Dill
Ducks egg
Dulse (seaweed)
Dyer's broom herb
Edam cheese
Eel smoked
Elderberries

Emmental cheese
Fennel
Fenugreek (Trigonella foenum-graecum)
Fernet Branca (herbal bitter liqueur)
Feta cheese
Fish innards
Fish pieces mixed (fresh water)
Fish sauce
Flounder
Flower pollen
Fox nut, gorgon nut, makhana
Fresh cheese from soya
Fresh cheese with herbs
Freshwater crab
Freshwater fish
Fructose (glucose)
Fruit mix juice
Fruit tea
Gail plum
Galangal
Garam Masala powder
Gelatin white
Gelee Royal
Gentian root
Gentian root tea
Ginkgo fruit
Ginseng
Ginseng liqueur
Ginseng root
Goat and sheep's blood
Goat and sheep's brain
Goat and sheep's liver
Goat and sheep's stomach
Goose blood
Goose fat
Gorgonzola
Gouda cheese
Grapefruit dried peel
Grapeseed oil
Grass carp
Greengage
Ground
Ground caraway
Guava
Halibut (Flatfish)
Hazelnuts
Herbal tea mix
Herbs bitter
Hibiscus
Hibiscus tea
Hijiki
Hokkaido pumpkin
Honey wine (Met)

Hop
Horehound leaves
Horse meat
Hyssop
Jasmine blossoms tee
Jellyfish
Juniper berry
Kaki plum
Kalmus
King Solomon's-seal
Kohlrabi
Kudzu
Kukicha tea
Ladyfingers
Lamb's lettuce
Lavender blossoms
Lemon Balm (dried)
Lemon Balm (fresh)
Lemongrass
Licorice root tea
Lily bulbs
Lime blossom tea
Linseed
Linseed (crushed)
Liver smoothing tea
Loquate / Japanese medlar
Lotus roots
Lotus seeds
Lovage
Lovage seeds
Luo Han Guo fruit
Lychee liqueur
Lye roll
Mango juice
Manioc flour
Mare's milk
Marjoram
Martini
Mascarpone cheese
Mayonnaise 50%
Mayonnaise 80%
Medlar
Mirabelle plum
Miso black (fermented)
Mixed Pickles
Mu Erh Mushroom
Muesli
Mulled Wine Spice
Multi-grain bread (gray bread)
Mustard
Mustard Dijon
Mustard medium hot
Mustard seeds
Mustard sweet

Nasturtium (nose-twister or nose-tweaker)
Nectarine
Nettles
Noodles (wheat) with egg
Noodles (wheat, lasagne) with egg
Noodles (wheat, ribbon noodles) with egg
Noodles (wheat, spaghetti) with egg
Noodles (whole grain) with egg
Nori, purple seaweed, red algae
Nutmeg
Oat flakes (whole grain)
Oat flour
Oat fusion (baby food)
Oat meal
Oat milk
Octopus
Olives green
Orange blossom
Orange dried peel
Orange grated peel
Orange jam
Orange peel
Oregano dried
Oregano fresh
Oyster shell powder
Palm oil
Parsley
Parsley root
Parsnip
Passion blossoms tea
Passion fruit
Peanut (roasted)
Peanut butter
Pearl barley
Pearl barley
Pepper (ground)
Pepper Cayenne
Pepper powder (hot)
Pepper white (ground)
Peppercorns
Peppermint
Peppermint tea
Pepperoni
Pepperoni, red, pitted, halved
Pepperoni, yellow, pitted, halved
Peppers (rose peppers)
Peppers (sweet)
Peppers powder
Perch
Pickle
Pig blood
Pigeon egg

Pine nuts
Plum dried
Plums
Pork Bacon
Pork brain
Pork fat (lard)
Pork ham
Pork ham cooked
Pork ham smoked
Pork Lard
Pork lung
Pork marrow bones
Pork sausage (Bratwurst)
Pork/beef sausage (smoked)
Pork's intestine
Potato (mealy)
Potato flour
Prickly pear
Processed cheese 12%
processed cheese 30%
Prosecco
Psyllium seed
Pudding powder vanilla
Puff pastry
Pumpernickel (dark bread)
Pumpkin seeds
Rabbit (wild)
Raisins
Raspberry jam
Raspberry leaf tea
Red beet
Red berry (without sugar)
Ribworttea
Rice (Gaoliang / Sorghum)
Rice (whole grain)
Rice flour
Rice mash
Rice round grain
Rice starch
Rice sticky
Rice sweet
Rice variety any
Rose blossom tea
Rose hip
Rose leaf tea
Rosemary
Rum
Rusk
Rye wholemeal bread
Safflower (Dyer's thistle / Hong Hua)
Salmon
Salt
Salt (herbal)
Savory

Savoy cabbage / kale
Sea buckthorn
Sea cucumber
Sesame oil roasted
Sesame paste (Tahini)
Sesame, black
Sesame, white
Sheep's milk
Sheep's milk yoghurt
Sherry (whine)
Shrimps
Skim milk powder
Slug
Sourdough
Soy flour
Soy noodles
Soy Tofu smoked
Soya Cuisine (soy cream)
Soybeans
Soybeans, blacks, fermented
Spelled (Dark) bread
Spelled semolina
Spelled wholemeal flour
Spurdog (spiny dogfish, Schillerlocken)
St. Benedict's thistle, blessed thistle,
holy thistle, spotted thistle
Star anise
Stevia (candyleaf, sweetleaf)
Strawberry jam
Sugar - icing sugar
Sugar palm sugar
Sugar substitute (sweetener)
Sunflower seeds
Supplementary nutrition
Tabasco
Tarragon (Estragon)
Tea mixture uric acid lowering
Thyme
Thyme dried
Toast bread (whole grain)
Tomato dried
Tomato juice
Tomato paste
Tomato puree
Tonic Water
Trout
Trout (smoked)
Truffle
Tuna
Turkey breast meat
Turkey ham
Turmeric (yellow root)
Turnip
Turnips

Umeboshi paste
Valerian
Vanilla
Vanilla pod
Vanilla powder
Vanilla sugar natural
Vinegar Aceto Balsamico white
Walnuts
Walnuts roasted
Water hot
Wax gourd
Wheat flatbread/pita bread
Wheat flour whole grain
Wheat/Rye/Gray-black bread with yeast
Wheatgrass juice
Whey
White bread (baguette)
White bread (pretzel sticks)

White bread (roll)
White bread (wheat bread)
White breadcrumbs
White cabbage
White dumpling bread (wheat bread cut into chunks)
Whitefish
Whole grain bread
Wholemeal flour
Wild garlic (garlic spinach)
Wild herbs
Wild strawberries
Wormwood herb
Yam root, yam root tuber
Yarrow
Yeast
Yew nut
Yoghurt vanilla

10.2 Use ingredients: yes

Almond marzipan
Almond milk
Almond puree
Anchovy / Sardine
Apple (sweet)
Apricot
Apricots
Arrowroot
Asparagus (green or white)
Aubergine
Basic recipe for a beef soup (warming)
Beef bone marrow
Beef heart
Beef kidney
Beef liver
Beef lungs (calf)
Beef meatbones
Beef stomach
Blackberry´s
Blueberry
Broccoli
Brussels sprouts
Calamari
Cashews
Cauliflower
Cherry
Chicken egg
Chicken heart
Chicken liver
Chicken stomach
Chinese cabbage
Coconut flakes
Coconut grated

Coconut milk
Cod
Coriander (fresh)
Corn
Couscous
Crucian
Eel
Fennel seeds ground
Fennel tea
Feta cheese
Fig
Fig dried
Goose
Goose egg
Goose parts
Gourd
Grape juice red
Grape juice white
Grapes red
Grapes white
Green spelt
Hawthorn
Herbs of Provence
Herbs various
Herbs wild
Herring
Kumquats
Lamb bones
Lamb kidneys
Lamb liver
Lamb meat
Lamb shoulder
Leek

Lobster
Longane
Lychee
Lychee in Preserved
Malt
Maple syrup
Miso
Morel (black, dried)
Octopus
Okra
Olives
Onion (shallot)
Onion (spring onion)
Onion read
Onion white
Oysters
Peaches
Peaches (canned)
Peanuts
Pear
Peas, green
Peppers
Pheasant
Pigeon
Pistachios
Plaice
Pomegranate
Poppy
Potato
Pumpkin
Quail
Quail egg
Quinoa
Radish (white, green, purple-red)
Radish black

Radish horseradish
Radish leaves
Raspberry
Red cabbage
Red wine
Rice (fragrance)
Rice Basmati
Rice black
Rice long grain rice
Rice malt
Rice noodles
Rice red
Rice wild (nature rice)
Rose hip tea
Rye
Rye flour
Saffron
Sago (cereals)
Salsify
Shark
Shrimp
Soy Tofu
Soybean milk
Soybeans, black
Soybeans, yellow
Spelled flakes
Spelled grain
Spinach
Spiny lobsters
Sugar molasses
Sweet potato
Topinambur
Water
White wine
Zucchini

10.3 Use ingredients: little

Adzuki beans
Apple (sour)
Apple juice (natural cloudy)
Artichoke
Balm
Bamboo shoots
Barley
Barley not peeled
Batavia
Bean oil
Beer (Top-fermented German dark beer)
Berry juice
Black beans
Black-eyed peas

Blueberry juice
Boletus mushroom
Borage oil
Broad beans (thick beans)
Buckwheat
Buckwheat (roasted) Kasha
Bulgur (cereals)
Bush beans
Butter beans white
Celery sticks
Chamomile
Champignon
Chanterelle
Cherry juice
Chickpeas

Chicory
Chocolate
Clementines
Coffee
Coix (seeds) YiYi Ren
Cooking oil
Cow's milk (1.5% fat)
Cow's milk (whole milk 3.5% fat)
Cranberry
Cranberry juice
Cress
Currant (black)
Currant (red)
Currant (white)
Curry
Curry paste red
Duck (heart)
Duck (slaughtered)
Elderberry blossom tee
Endive salad
Evening primrose oil
Fish remains
French beans
Fresh cheese
Garlic
Ginger fresh
Ginger oil
Ginger powder
Goat
Goat and sheep's milk
Goat cheese
Gooseberry
Grapefruit (Pomelo)
Grapefruit juice
Green tea
Honey
Iceberg lettuce
Kidney beans (red)
Lamb's lettuce
Leaf salads (bitter)
Lemon peel
Lentils
Lentils black
Lentils red
Lentils yellow
Lettuce
Lima beans
Linseed oil
Mackerel
Mallow (Malva sylvestris) blossom tea
Margarine
Margarine (diet)
Miso paste (soy bean paste)
Mold cheese

Morel, dried
Mozzarella
Mung bean
Mung bean sprouting
Mutton
Mutton
Olive oil
Oyster mushroom
Parmesan
Peanut oil
Pear juice
Peas
Pimento
Pinto beans speckled
Pork heart
Pork kidneys
Pork knuckle
Pork liver
Pork meat
Pork skin
Pork stomach
Pumpkin seed oil
Quince
Rabbit
Rabbit liver
Rabbit meat
Radicchio
Radish
Rapeseed oil
Raspberry dried (immature)
Reishi mushroom
Romaine lettuce / lettuce salad
Rosefish
Rucola
Sage
Sauerkraut (cutted cabbage fermented)
Sesame oil
Shiitake, dried
Sour cherries
Soy sauce
Soybean oil
Spirit
Strawberries
Strawberry Juice
Sugar brown
Sugar candy white
Sugar cane sugar
Sugar fructose - fruit sugar
Sugar glucose - grapes sugar
Sugar Milk Sugar
Sugar white
Sunflower oil
Tangerine
Thistle oil

Tsampa (roasted barley flour)
Umeboshi plums (Japanese apricots)
Vegetable juice
Vinegar (Apple vinegar)
Vinegar (Red wine vinegar)
Vinegar Aceto Balsamico

Walnut oil
Wheat germ oil
White beans
Wild boar meat
Wormwood

10.4 Do not use contra-acting foods

Agar agar (kelp)
Amaranth
Avocado
Banana
Banana (cooking banana)
Basic recipe for a duck soup
Beer (Pils)
Black tea
Burdock root tea
Butter organic
Buttermilk
Cantaloupe
Carambola (Star fruit)
Caviar
Chard
Chlorella (fresh water)
Crab
Cream, sweet 30%
Créme fraiche cheese
Cucumber
Curd cheese 20%
Curd cheese 40%
Dandelion (young plants)
Dandelionroots tea
Deer meat
Deer meat
Kefir
Kiwi
Kombu seaweed (Saccharina japonica)
Lemon
Lemon juice
Lime
Mango
Mediterranean fish (cod, plaice,
haddock, sea
Millet
Millet flakes

Mineral water
Mulberry fruit
Mullet
Mussels
Oat
Oat flakes roasted
Orange
Orange juice
Papaya
Pineapple
Pineapple (from a can)
Pineapple juice without sugar
Plum
Rhubarb
Sake
Seacrab
Sorrel
Sour cream 15% fat
Sour milk
Sour milk cheese 20%
Tomato
Wakame
Watermelon
Wheat
Wheat beer
Wheat bran
Wheat bulgur
Wheat flakes
Wheat flour
Wheat semolina
Wheat semolina for children
Wheatgrass powder
Yarrow tea
Yogi tea
Yogurt (natural, 1.5% fat)
Yogurt (natural, 3.5% fat)

11 Herbs and their effects

11.1 Basil

thermal effect: warm
taste: spicy, bitter
Dries out, leads down. Tonifies Yang and Qi, dissolves mucus-cold, eliminates wind-cold.
It has a beneficial effect on flatulence and nausea, relaxing and soothing. Good to fight emphysema, bronchitis, whooping cough, high blood pressure, headache, mouth odor, warts, hiccup, gout, migraine.

11.2 Mugwort

thermal effect: warm
taste: bitter, spicy
Regulates and nourishes bleeding, warms the inside, eliminates wind-cold, eliminates parasites, eliminates heat, wetness, regulates and moves Qi.
Reduces bleeding, alleviates pain. In the kitchen, mugwort is used as a spice for fat food. Since it contains many bitter substances, it boosts fat burning and promotes digestion.

11.3 Savory

thermal effect: warm
taste: bitter
Tonifies kidney yang, heart qi, stomach and spleen qi and warms the middle, moves the liver qi and blood, releases mucous and cold from the lungs, opens the surface, induces wind-cold.
Stomach-strengthening, soothing and appetizing. Ideal for prevent colds, strengthens the immune system. In case of incontinence or nocturnal wetting (not for children), put the beans in liquor for libido.

11.4 Dill

thermal effect: warm
taste: spicy
Moves qi, triggers stagnation, heads up.
The medicinal and spice herb has an antispasmodic effect and stimulates gastric juice production. Good to fight flatulence. Antispasmodic for gastrointestinal discomfort.

11.5 Coriander

thermal effect: warm
taste: spicy
Driving sweat, reducing wind, draining moisture, tonifying and regulating qi, eliminating wind-cold.
The essential oils are appetizing, digestive, cramping and soothing in stomach and intestinal disorders.

11.6 Herbs various

Stimulates appetite. Effect different.
Appetizing, lots of trace elements and vitamins.

11.7 Cress

thermal effect: cool
taste: sweet
Moves and tonifies qi and blood, diuretic, cools in internal heat, moisturizes lungs, triggers stagnation, heads upwards.
Diuretic, supports urination. Good to fight dry mouth, inner agitation, sore throat, diabetes, kidney stones, gastrointestinal complaints, lung problems, menstrual cramps or cancer.

11.8 Chives

thermal effect: warm
taste: spicy
Directs upward. Tonifies blood, kidney Yang and Qi. Dissolves moisture.
Bactericide, prevents cancer, strengthens gastric juice production, promotes digestion and blood circulation, promotes growth, triggers stagnation.

11.9 Lovage

thermal effect: warm
taste: spicy, bitter
Reduces inner wind and moisture, dissolves stagnation, directs upward, warms Yang, regulates and moves Qi, warms inside, dissolves mucus-cold, eliminates wind-cold.
Stimulates digestion, reduces pain. Extracts of the root are used to flush out urinary tract infections and prevent kidney gravel.

11.10 Lily bulbs

thermal effect: cool
taste: sweet, bitter
Tonifies Yin, soothes Shen / Spirit. Moisturizes the lungs, clears heat and stops coughing.
Calms nerves, good to fight scaly skin. The onions and the petals are added to ointments in the Orient, which can heal muscles and tendons.
White lily (astringent).

11.11 Oregano fresh

thermal effect: warm
taste: bitter
Dries out, directs down, regulates and moves Qi, eliminates wind-cold, soothes Shen / Spirit, suppresses inner wind, warms inside, eliminates wind-cold / heat-wetness, moves blood, dissolves slime-cold.
It has an anti-digestive, calming and nerve-strengthening effect, helps to fight cramping stomach and intestinal disorders. The ingredient Carvacrol has an anti-inflammatory effect.

11.12 Parsley

thermal effect: warm
taste: bitter
Nourishes blood and liver, harmonizes liver and spleen, strengthens eyesight, preserves juices, contracts. Dissolves moisture and warms Yang.
Stimulates liver function, detoxifies. Forces urinating. Relieves flatulence. Digestive and menstrual stimulating, birth-accelerating, memory-enhancing, blood-purifying, skin-smoothing.

11.13 Peppermint

thermal effect: cool
taste: spicy, bitter
Cools heat, expels mucus, dissipates wind-cold and wind-heat, moves stomach qi, releases congestion, tonifies, regulates and moves qi.
Relaxes, frees the lungs and the nose (inhale), regulates the cycle.
Stimulates bile flow and bile production, antispasmodic in gastrointestinal disorders, antimicrobial and antiviral.

11.14   Rosemary

thermal effect: warm
taste: bitter
Dries out, leads down. Strengthens the heart, lungs and spleen qi,
strengthens liver blood. Strengthens heart-Yin.
Expels spleen heat / cold moisture. Strengthens spleen and kidney yang.
Promotes digestion, relieves bloating, strengthens lung, spleen and
kidney. Affects the circulation and nerves.
Appetizing. Baths help to fight circulatory disorders as well as with gout
and rheumatism.

11.15   Sage

thermal effect: neutral
taste: bitter, spicy
Expels slime, guides down, strengthens Qi, eliminates Wind-Heat,
abstrating, eliminate heat induced by Yin deficiency.
Good to fight yeast infections. The leaves have a digestive effect and are
used in greasy foods. Antiperspirant effect.
Helps to relieve coughing attacks. Dries out.

11.16   Black caraway

thermal effect: warm
taste: spicy, sweet
Dissolve / transform moisture, tonifyes Yang and Qi, moves blood,
suppresses inner wind.
Detoxifying, immunoregulatory. In addition, the oil should stimulate the
formation of bone marrow cells and generally protect body cells from
viruses.

11.17   Thyme dried

thermal effect: warm
taste: bitter
Strengthens the lungs and spleen. Clears wind-cold, dissolves slime-cold,
tones qi, soothes Shen / Spirit.
Disinfecting. It stimulates the blood circulation, increases the appetite and
helps to digest fat meat better.

11.18   King Solomon's-seal

thermal effect: neutral

taste: sweet, bitter
Tonifies Yin and Qi, astringent, tonifies blood, eliminates wind-cold / heat-wetness.
Used to repair wounds or damaged tissue. Good to fight dry cough, earlier also tuberculosis and dysentery, as well as diarrhea and hemorrhoids.

11.19 Yam root, yam root tuber

thermal effect: neutral
taste: sweet
Tonifies Yin, Yang and Qi, reduces inner wind, dissolves wetness, warms Yang.
Solves cramps (in the gastrointestinal tract). Digestive through increased bile production. Anti-inflammatory in rheumatic diseases.
Mucolytic agent for coughing. Relief of menopausal symptoms.

11.20 Lemongrass

thermal effect: taste:
Diverting, calming.
Reduction of flatulence, antimicrobial, appetizing. Prevention of influenza.
Good to fight infections in the mouth and
throat.

11.21 Lemon Balm (fresh)

thermal effect: cool
taste: sour
Soothes Shen / Spirit, regulates and moves Qi, eliminates heat caused by Yin deficiency, tones Qi.
Stimulating, antibacterial, encouraging, relaxing, antispasmodic, cooling, antipyretic, analgesic, sweat-inducing, virus-inhibiting. Good for colds, fever, flu, cough, bronchitis, asthma, loss of appetite, bloating, heartburn.

12 Basics of Nutrition

The basic principles of nutrition described herein are general recommendations. They are not aimed at a specific form of therapy. Recommendations concerning a therapy have priority.

12.1 Nutrition

Regular meals in a relaxed atmosphere. A warm breakfast is considered a good start into the day.

The main meals ought to be taken for lunch – supper in the early evening. Pay attention to feeling hungry or sated: don't eat too much nor remain hungry is the rule

Prepare the meals freshly from natural, regional products. Frozen, heat-conserved, industrially prepared or foodstuffs cooked in the microwave oven are rejected.

Choice of foodstuffs according to the season: more cooling food in summer, more warming food in winter.

Eat cooked food at least twice a day. Food and drinks ought to be lukewarm, never ice-cold or hot.

Raw vegetables, briefly cooked vegetables, freshly squeezed juices and mineral water are not recommended. Milk and dairy products are only included in the diet if they don't cause problems. Don't use therapeutic recipes over a longer period without consulting your doctor or therapist.

Varied food

Enjoy the diversity of foodstuffs. Characteristics of a balanced nutrition are variety, suitable combination and a balanced quantity of rich and low energy foodstuffs (on one hand avoiding undersupply with essential nutrients and on the other hand to take to many undesirable substances).

A lot of Cereal Products - and Potatoes

Bread, pasta, rice, cereal flakes (best wholemeal) as well as potatoes contain almost no fat, but many vitamins, mineral nutrients, trace elements, roughage and secondary plant substances. These foodstuffs ought to be taken with low-fat side dishes.

Vegetables and Fruit – „Take Five" every day ... 5 portions of vegetables and fruit a day, as fresh as possible, briefly cooked, or maybe one portion as a juice – ideal as a side dish to every meal as well as snack between meals: Thus a lot of vitamins, mineral nutrients as well as roughage and secondary plant substances

Daily milk and dairy products
Milk and Dairy Products every Day, once or twice per Week Fish; meat, sausages as well as eggs moderately. These foodstuffs contain valuable nutrients like calcium in the milk, iodine selenium and omega-3 fat acids in saltwater fish. Meat is favorable due to its high content of disposable iron and the vitamins B1, B6 and B12. Quantities of 300 – 600 g meat and sausage per week are sufficient. Prefer low-fat products, especially in meat- and dairy products.

Low-fat and fatty Foodstuffs
Fat supplies us with essential fat acids and fatty foodstuffs contain also fat-soluble vitamins. Fat is high in energy; therefore much fat in the food may cause overweight, possibly also cancer. Too many saturated fat acids may further a tendency for cardio-vascular diseases in the long term. Prefer vegetable oils and fats (e.g. rapeseed-, olive-, soya-oils and solid fats produced therefrom). Beware of invisible fat in meat- and dairy products, pastry and sweets as well as in fast-food and convenience foods. 70 – 90 g fat per day is sufficient.

Moderately Sugar and Salt
Take sugar and foods/drinks containing various kinds of sugar (e.g. glucose syrup) only occasionally. Use herbs and spices as well as a little salt creatively. Prefer salt containing iodine.

Plenty of Liquids
Water is absolutely essential. Drink 1-2 l liquids every day. Prefer water (with or without gas) and other low-calorie drinks. Alcoholic drinks should not be taken.

Tasty Dishes, carefully cooked
Cook the meals with as low temperatures and as short as possible, using little water and fat – this preserves the original taste, keeps the nutrients intact and prevents the production of harmful compounds.

Take time and enjoy the food
Take your Time and enjoy your Food
Eating consciously helps to eat right. The eye enjoys food, too. It's fun, invites to enjoy varied dishes and stimulates the feeling of satiety.

Watch your Weight and stay in Motion
A balanced diet and a lot of exercise and sport (30 – 60 min/day) are a healthy combination. The right weight furthers well-being and health. Thermals, directional effectiveness, digestive power

There are various criteria for judging the effectiveness of herbs and foodstuffs.
The use of certain herbs and ingredients is based on observations of the effects on the body which these foodstuffs, herbs and spices show after having eaten them. The medical science has developed following system: Every ingredient or herb has a directional effectiveness. Furthermore, there are herbs which have a special effect on certain organs.
The basic condition for a healthy metabolism is to obtain sufficient energy from food and that the digestive process doesn't use too much energy. An easily digestible meal makes content and sated, doesn't cause flatulence and fatigue after the meal. The perfect spices increase the healthiness of our meals. Very often, just small doses of herbs and spices will suffice. They are not used to make us sated, but to help our digestive organs to digest the food.

12.2 Recipes

The recipes list the ingredients to be used and the cooking instructions show how the dish is prepared. The list of ingredients shows the concerned quantities as well as the relevance for the therapy. If you find „less than mentioned", try to comply or find an alternative from the „list of recommended foodstuffs". Mostly it shall result just in a small change of taste when you simply avoid this ingredient.
Mild cooking methods: boiling, stewing, poaching, steaming
Strong cooking methods: barbecuing, roasting, frying, smoking
Balanced cooking methods: deep-frying, baking brick
Deep-freezing and warming in the microwave oven should be avoided (denaturalization).

12.3 Foodstuffs

Foodstuffs have an effect on body and soul like medicinal herbs, only a very much milder one. Dietary advice is mainly based on regional foodstuffs. The knowledge about the effects of each foodstuff and the knowledge, when which foodstuff shall be used, is based on the orthodox school of medicine. Use ecologic-organic products, if possible. As everything should be cooked for a long time due to a better digestability and very rarely eaten raw, the food agrees with everyone.
The classification of the foodstuffs according to their effect on the body is the basis in order to achieve a harmonious status of health.
Dietary advisors do not recommend certain foodstuffs for everyone. The individual diet is tailor-made for the individual constitution.

Buy only fresh and ripe fruit and vegetables. You ought to leave unripe fruit and vegetables and such with brown spots and wilted leaves behind in the market. In this case take deep-frozen goods (never ready-to-serve dishes!). Fruit and vegetables are deep-frozen immediately after harvesting and often contain more vitamins and minerals than the goods from the vegetable shelf. Whereas conserved or tinned goods contain very much less biological substances. Also, salt, sugar and others are mostly added to the latter. Never leave the foodstuffs in the water after washing them to avoid that many vital substances get drowned. Clean salads, fruit and vegetables immediately before serving.

Please make sure of the hygienic processing of foodstuffs. Clean your salads, fruit and vegetables carefully. When cooking with meat, prepare all ingredients first and then process the meat products. Clean the worktop and tools very carefully. Wooden surfaces ought to be treated with a mild disinfectant regularly in order to reduce germination.
Store fruit and vegetables separately, if possible. Harvested fruit and vegetables are still alive and emit e.g. ethylene gas, which makes other products ripen and age faster. Keep meat and fish in the closed packaging or store them in the fridge in closed containers.

12.4 Herbs

There are some basic rules for storing medicinal herbs. On principle, herbs must be protected from direct sunlight, humidity and heat.

Containers for the storage of herbs may be glasses, ceramic jars and even plastic containers. However, plastic is a rather unsuitable material and should only be a short-term solution. In case of glass containers, use a dark material.

Medicinal herbs cannot be kept for any long period. The shelf life of herbs is limited. However, it can be prolonged with suitable storage. The place should be dark, rather cool and absolutely dry. A wooden medicine cabinet, placed not directly next to a source of heat, would be ideal. Never buy large quantities of herbs so as not to have to throw them away. Label the container with the name of the herb and the date of harvesting or processing.

13 Other dietic-books

The following syndromes of dietetics, TCM or for a therapy supplement for cancer are available.

Dietetics

E001. Nutrition of the infant - baby food
E002. Nutrition during lactation
E003. Nutrition in old age
E004. Nutrition of children and adolescents
E005. Nutrition of athletes
E006. Light weight
E007. Pregnancy
E008. Full food

Protein and electrolyte - kidneys
E009. (hemodialysis) dialysis treatment
E010. Acute renal failure
E011. Chronic renal insufficiency
E012. Nephrotic syndrome
E013. Kidney stones (nephrolithiasis)

Gastrointestinal tract - pancreas
E014. Acute pancreatitis (inflammation of the pancreas)
E015. Chronic pancreatitis (inflammation of the pancreas)

Gastrointestinal tract - small intestine and large intestine
E016. Acute obstipation (constipation)
E017. Chronic obstipation (constipation)
E018. Colon irritabile
E019. Diverticulitis
E020. Acquired lactose intolerance (lactose malabsorption)
E021. Fructose malabsorption
E022. Glutensensitive enteropathy (celiac disease)
E023. Colectomy
E024. Short Bowel Syndrome

Gastrointestinal tract - liver, gallbladder, bile ducts
E025. Acute and chronic hepatitis (inflammation of the liver)
E026. Cholelithiasis (bile stones)
E027. fatty liver
E028. cirrhosis

Gastrointestinal tract - Stomach and duodenal intestine
E029. Acute gastritis
E030. Chronic gastritis
E031. Stomach bleeding
E032. Ulcus ventriculi and duodenal ulcer
E033. Condition after gastric surgery

Gastrointestinal tract - oral cavity and esophagus
E034. Stomatitis
E035. Esophageal carcinoma (esophageal cancer)
E036. Refluosophagitis (heartburn)

Special diseases
E037. Phenylketonuria (PKU)
E038. Rheumatic joint diseases

Metabolism
E039. Obesity (overweight)
E040. Diabetes mellitus
E041. Eating disorders (underweight)

Fat metabolism
E042. Hypercholesterolaemia (increased cholesterol level)
E043. Hepatic Encephalopathy

Heart and circulation
E044. Arteriosclerosis (arterial calcification)
E045. Heart insufficiency
E046. Hypertension
E047. Hyperuricaemia and gout

Changed nutrient requirements
E048. In case of fever
E049. For malignant diseases
E050. After burns
E051. Radiation and chemotherapy

CANCER
E100. Pancreatic cancer
E101. Bladder cancer
E102. Blood cancer (leukemia)
E103. Breast cancer
E104. Colorectal cancer
E105. Gastric cancer
E106. Kidney cancer
E107. Esophageal cancer

TCM
E200. Bladder - moisture heat in the bladder
E201. Bladder - moisture and cold in the bladder
E202. Bladder - emptiness and cold in the bladder
E203. Large intestine - external cold affects the large intestine
E204. Large intestine - moisture heat in the large intestine
E205. Large intestine - heat blocks the intestine II acute
E206. Large intestine - dryness of the colon
E207. Large intestine - Yang deficiency (cold)
E208. Heart - Blood insufficiency
E209. Heart - Blood stagnation
E210. Heart - Fire
E211. Heart - Hot mucus clogs the heart pores

E212. Heart - Cold mucus clogs the heart pores
E213. Heart - Qi deficiency
E214. Heart - Yang deficiency
E215. Heart - Yin deficiency
E216. Liver - Ascending Liver Yang
E217. Liver - Blood deficiency
E218. Liver - Blood stagnation
E219. Liver - Moisture heat in liver and gall bladder
E220. Liver - Fire
E221. Liver - Gall bladder Qi-Empty
E222. Liver - Cold in the liver meridian
E223. Liver - Qi stagnation
E224. Liver - Wind
E225. Liver - Wind with ascending liver Yang
E226. Liver - Wind with blood anemic
E227. Liver - Wind with extreme heat
E228. Lung - Qi deficiency
E229. Lung - Mucus-moisture in the lungs
E230. Lung - Mucus-heat in the lungs
E231. Lung - Mucus-cold in the lungs
E232. Lung - Dryness of the lungs
E233. Lung - Wind-heat attacks the lungs
E234. Lung - Wind-cold affects the lungs
E235. Lung - Yin deficiency
E236. Stomach - Bloodstagnation
E237. Stomach - Fire
E238. Stomach - Cold with liquid
E239. Stomach - Nutrition stagnation
E240. Stomach - Qi deficiency
E241. Stomach - Rebellious Qi
E242. Stomach - Yin Emptiness
E243. Spleen - Heat and moisture attack the spleen
E244. Spleen - Coldness and moisture affects the spleen
E245. Spleen - Qi deficiency
E246. Spleen - Qi deficiency + Declining spleen Qi
E247. Spleen - Qi deficiency + spleen does not control the blood
E248. Spleen - Yang deficiency
E249. Kidney - Heart and kidney no longer communicate
E250. Kidney - Jing deficiency
E251. Kidney - Kidneys cannot receive the Qi
E252. Kidney - Qi is not stable
E253. Kidney - Yang deficiency
E254. Kidney - Yin deficiency

For further information visit di-book.com.